NUCLEAR POSTURE REVIEW REPORT

APRIL 2010

Nuclear Posture Review Report

April 2010

CONTENTS

PREFACE ... i

EXECUTIVE SUMMARY ... iii

INTRODUCTION ... 1

THE CHANGED – AND CHANGING –
NUCLEAR SECURITY ENVIRONMENT ... 3

PREVENTING NUCLEAR PROLIFERATION
AND NUCLEAR TERRORISM ... 9

REDUCING THE ROLE OF U.S. NUCLEAR WEAPONS ... 15

MAINTAINING STRATEGIC DETERRENCE AND
STABILITY AT REDUCED NUCLEAR FORCE LEVELS ... 19

STRENGTHENING REGIONAL DETERRENCE
AND REASSURING U.S. ALLIES AND PARTNERS ... 31

SUSTAINING A SAFE, SECURE,
AND EFFECTIVE NUCLEAR ARSENAL ... 37

LOOKING AHEAD:
TOWARD A WORLD WITHOUT NUCLEAR WEAPONS ... 45

SECRETARY OF DEFENSE
1000 DEFENSE PENTAGON
WASHINGTON, DC 20301-1000

April 6, 2010

This Nuclear Posture Review provides a roadmap for implementing President Obama's agenda for reducing nuclear risks to the United States, our allies and partners, and the international community. As the President said in Prague last year, a world without nuclear weapons will not be achieved quickly, but we must begin to take concrete steps today.

This NPR places the prevention of nuclear terrorism and proliferation at the top of the U.S. policy agenda, and describes how the United States will reduce the role and numbers of nuclear weapons. Efforts like the New Strategic Arms Reduction Treaty with Russia, the Nuclear Security Summit, our work to strengthen the nuclear nonproliferation regime, and a broader approach to deterrence are central elements of this strategy.

At the same time, as long as nuclear weapons exist, the United States must sustain a safe, secure, and effective nuclear arsenal – to maintain strategic stability with other major nuclear powers, deter potential adversaries, and reassure our allies and partners of our security commitments to them.

The NPR calls for making much-needed investments to rebuild America's aging nuclear infrastructure. To this end, I asked for nearly $5 billion to be transferred from the Department of Defense to the Department of Energy over the next several years. These investments, and the NPR's strategy for warhead life extension, represent a credible modernization plan necessary to sustain the nuclear infrastructure and support our nation's deterrent. They will also enable further arms reductions by allowing us to hedge against future threats without the need for a large non-deployed stockpile.

From beginning to end, this review was an interagency effort, and as such reflects the strength of what can be accomplished when our government's departments work in concert. The steps outlined in this report will take years, and, in some cases, decades to complete. Implementing them will be the work of multiple administrations and Congresses, and will require sustained bipartisan consensus.

In closing, I would like to thank those men and women at the Departments of Defense and Energy, including the national labs, who are critical to sustaining our nuclear arsenal. Their important work underwrites the security of the United States as well as our partners and allies.

EXECUTIVE SUMMARY

In his April 2009 speech in Prague, President Obama highlighted 21st century nuclear dangers, declaring that to overcome these grave and growing threats, the United States will "seek the peace and security of a world without nuclear weapons." He recognized that such an ambitious goal could not be reached quickly – perhaps, he said, not in his lifetime. But the President expressed his determination to take concrete steps toward that goal, including by reducing the number of nuclear weapons and their role in U.S. national security strategy. At the same time, he pledged that as long as nuclear weapons exist, the United States will maintain a safe, secure, and effective arsenal, both to deter potential adversaries and to assure U.S. allies and other security partners that they can count on America's security commitments.

President Barack Obama unveils his vision for reducing nuclear dangers and pursuing the long-term goal of a world without nuclear weapons in Prague's Hradcany Square on Apr. 5, 2009. Official White House photo by Lawrence Jackson.

The 2010 Nuclear Posture Review (NPR) outlines the Administration's approach to promoting the President's agenda for reducing nuclear dangers and pursuing the goal of a world without nuclear weapons, while simultaneously advancing broader U.S. security interests. The NPR reflects the President's national security priorities and the supporting defense strategy objectives identified in the 2010 Quadrennial Defense Review.

After describing fundamental changes in the international security environment, the NPR report focuses on five key objectives of our nuclear weapons policies and posture:

1. Preventing nuclear proliferation and nuclear terrorism;

2. Reducing the role of U.S. nuclear weapons in U.S. national security strategy;

3. Maintaining strategic deterrence and stability at reduced nuclear force levels;

4. Strengthening regional deterrence and reassuring U.S. allies and partners; and

5. Sustaining a safe, secure, and effective nuclear arsenal.

While the NPR focused principally on steps to be taken in the next five to ten years, it also considered the path ahead for U.S. nuclear strategy and posture over the longer term. Making sustained progress to reduce nuclear dangers, while ensuring security for ourselves and our allies and partners, will require a concerted effort by a long succession of U.S. Administrations and Congresses. Forging a sustainable consensus on the way ahead is critical.

The Changed – and Changing – International Security Environment

The international security environment has changed dramatically since the end of the Cold War. The threat of global nuclear war has become remote, but the risk of nuclear attack has increased.

As President Obama has made clear, today's most immediate and extreme danger is nuclear terrorism. Al Qaeda and their extremist allies are seeking nuclear weapons. We must assume they would use such weapons if they managed to obtain them. The vulnerability to theft or seizure of vast stocks of such nuclear materials around the world, and the availability of sensitive equipment and technologies in the nuclear black market, create a serious risk that terrorists may acquire what they need to build a nuclear weapon.

Today's other pressing threat is nuclear proliferation. Additional countries – especially those at odds with the United States, its allies and partners, and the broader international community – may acquire nuclear weapons. In pursuit of their nuclear ambitions, North Korea and Iran have violated non-proliferation obligations, defied directives of the United Nations Security Council, pursued missile delivery capabilities, and resisted international efforts to resolve through diplomatic means the crises they have created. Their provocative behavior has increased instability in their regions and could generate pressures in neighboring countries for considering nuclear deterrent options of their own. Continued non-compliance with non-proliferation norms by these and other countries would seriously weaken the Nuclear Non-Proliferation Treaty (NPT), with adverse security implications for the United States and the international community.

While facing the increasingly urgent threats of nuclear terrorism and nuclear proliferation, the United States must continue to address the more familiar challenge of ensuring strategic stability with existing nuclear powers – most notably Russia and China. Russia remains America's only peer in the area of nuclear weapons capabilities. But the nature of the U.S.-Russia relationship has changed fundamentally since the days of the Cold War. While policy differences continue to arise between the two countries and Russia continues to modernize its still-formidable nuclear forces, Russia and the United States are no longer adversaries, and prospects for military confrontation have declined dramatically. The two have increased their cooperation in areas of shared interest, including preventing nuclear terrorism and nuclear proliferation.

EXECUTIVE SUMMARY

The United States and China are increasingly interdependent and their shared responsibilities for addressing global security threats, such as weapons of mass destruction (WMD) proliferation and terrorism, are growing. At the same time, the United States and China's Asian neighbors remain concerned about China's current military modernization efforts, including its qualitative and quantitative modernization of its nuclear arsenal. China's nuclear arsenal remains much smaller than the arsenals of Russia and the United States. But the lack of transparency surrounding its nuclear programs – their pace and scope, as well as the strategy and doctrine that guides them – raises questions about China's future strategic intentions.

These changes in the nuclear threat environment have altered the hierarchy of our nuclear concerns and strategic objectives. In coming years, we must give top priority to discouraging additional countries from acquiring nuclear weapons capabilities and stopping terrorist groups from acquiring nuclear bombs or the materials to build them. At the same time, we must continue to maintain stable strategic relationships with Russia and China and counter threats posed by any emerging nuclear-armed states, thereby protecting the United States and our allies and partners against nuclear threats or intimidation, and reducing any incentives they might have to seek their own nuclear deterrents.

Implications for U.S. Nuclear Weapons Policies and Force Posture

The massive nuclear arsenal we inherited from the Cold War era of bipolar military confrontation is poorly suited to address the challenges posed by suicidal terrorists and unfriendly regimes seeking nuclear weapons. Therefore, it is essential that we better align our nuclear policies and posture to our most urgent priorities – preventing nuclear terrorism and nuclear proliferation.

This does not mean that our nuclear deterrent has become irrelevant. Indeed, as long as nuclear weapons exist, the United States will sustain safe, secure, and effective nuclear forces. These nuclear forces will continue to play an essential role in deterring potential adversaries and reassuring allies and partners around the world.

But fundamental changes in the international security environment in recent years – including the growth of unrivaled U.S. conventional military capabilities, major improvements in missile defenses, and the easing of Cold War rivalries – enable us to fulfill those objectives at significantly lower nuclear force levels and with reduced reliance on nuclear weapons. Therefore, without jeopardizing our traditional deterrence and reassurance goals, we are now able to shape our nuclear weapons policies and force structure in ways that will better enable us to meet our most pressing security challenges.

- By reducing the role and numbers of U.S. nuclear weapons – meeting our NPT Article VI obligation to make progress toward nuclear disarmament – we can put ourselves in a much stronger position to persuade our NPT partners to join with us in adopting the measures needed to reinvigorate the non-proliferation regime and secure nuclear materials worldwide.

- By maintaining a credible nuclear deterrent and reinforcing regional security architectures with missile defenses and other conventional military capabilities, we can reassure our non-nuclear allies and partners worldwide of our security commitments to them and confirm that they do not need nuclear weapons capabilities of their own.

- By pursuing a sound Stockpile Management Program for extending the life of U.S. nuclear weapons, we can ensure a safe, secure, and effective deterrent without the development of new nuclear warheads or further nuclear testing.

- By modernizing our aging nuclear facilities and investing in human capital, we can substantially reduce the number of nuclear weapons we retain as a hedge against technical or geopolitical surprise, accelerate dismantlement of retired warheads, and improve our understanding of foreign nuclear weapons activities.

- By promoting strategic stability with Russia and China and improving transparency and mutual confidence, we can help create the conditions for moving toward a world without nuclear weapons and build a stronger basis for addressing nuclear proliferation and nuclear terrorism.

- By working to reduce the salience of nuclear weapons in international affairs and moving step-by-step toward eliminating them, we can reverse the growing expectation that we are destined to live in a world with more nuclear-armed states, and decrease incentives for additional countries to hedge against an uncertain future by pursuing nuclear options of their own.

Preventing Nuclear Proliferation and Nuclear Terrorism

As a critical element of our effort to move toward a world free of nuclear weapons, the United States will lead expanded international efforts to rebuild and strengthen the global nuclear non-proliferation regime – and for the first time, the 2010 NPR places this priority atop the U.S. nuclear agenda. Concerns have grown in recent years that we are approaching a nuclear tipping point – that unless today's dangerous trends are arrested and reversed, before very long we will be living in a world with a steadily growing number of nuclear-armed states and an increasing likelihood of terrorists getting their hands on nuclear weapons.

The U.S. approach to preventing nuclear proliferation and nuclear terrorism includes three key elements. First, we seek to bolster the nuclear non-proliferation regime and its centerpiece, the NPT, by reversing the nuclear ambitions of North Korea and Iran, strengthening International

Atomic Energy Agency safeguards and enforcing compliance with them, impeding illicit nuclear trade, and promoting the peaceful uses of nuclear energy without increasing proliferation risks. Second, we are accelerating efforts to implement President Obama's initiative to secure all vulnerable nuclear materials worldwide in four years.

And third, we are pursuing arms control efforts – including the New Strategic Arms Reduction Treaty (New START), ratification and entry into force of the Comprehensive Nuclear Test Ban Treaty, and negotiation of a verifiable Fissile Material Cutoff Treaty – as a means of strengthening our ability to mobilize broad international support for the measures needed to reinforce the non-proliferation regime and secure nuclear materials worldwide.

Among key Administration initiatives are:

- Pursuing aggressively the President's Prague initiative to secure all vulnerable nuclear materials worldwide, including accelerating the Global Threat Reduction Initiative and the International Nuclear Material Protection and Cooperation Program. This includes increasing funding in fiscal year (FY) 2011 for Department of Energy nuclear non-proliferation programs to $2.7 billion, more than 25 percent.

- Enhancing national and international capabilities to disrupt illicit proliferation networks and interdict smuggled nuclear materials, and continuing to expand our nuclear forensics efforts to improve the ability to identify the source of nuclear material used or intended for use in a terrorist nuclear explosive device.

- Initiating a comprehensive national research and development program to support continued progress toward a world free of nuclear weapons, including expanded work on verification technologies and the development of transparency measures.

- Renewing the U.S. commitment to hold fully accountable any state, terrorist group, or other non-state actor that supports or enables terrorist efforts to obtain or use weapons of mass destruction, whether by facilitating, financing, or providing expertise or safe haven for such efforts.

Reducing the Role of U.S. Nuclear Weapons

The role of nuclear weapons in U.S. national security and U.S. military strategy has been reduced significantly in recent decades, but further steps can and should be taken at this time.

The fundamental role of U.S. nuclear weapons, which will continue as long as nuclear weapons exist, is to deter nuclear attack on the United States, our allies, and partners.

During the Cold War, the United States reserved the right to use nuclear weapons in response to a massive conventional attack by the Soviet Union and its Warsaw Pact allies. Moreover, after the

United States gave up its own chemical and biological weapons (CBW) pursuant to international treaties (while some states continue to possess or pursue them), it reserved the right to employ nuclear weapons to deter CBW attack on the United States and its allies and partners.

Since the end of the Cold War, the strategic situation has changed in fundamental ways. With the advent of U.S. conventional military preeminence and continued improvements in U.S. missile defenses and capabilities to counter and mitigate the effects of CBW, the role of U.S. nuclear weapons in deterring non-nuclear attacks – conventional, biological, or chemical – has declined significantly. The United States will continue to reduce the role of nuclear weapons in deterring non-nuclear attacks.

To that end, the United States is now prepared to strengthen its long-standing "negative security assurance" by declaring that the United States will not use or threaten to use nuclear weapons against non-nuclear weapons states that are party to the NPT and in compliance with their nuclear non-proliferation obligations.

This revised assurance is intended to underscore the security benefits of adhering to and fully complying with the NPT and persuade non-nuclear weapon states party to the Treaty to work with the United States and other interested parties to adopt effective measures to strengthen the non-proliferation regime.

In making this strengthened assurance, the United States affirms that any state eligible for the assurance that uses chemical or biological weapons against the United States or its allies and partners would face the prospect of a devastating conventional military response – and that any individuals responsible for the attack, whether national leaders or military commanders, would be held fully accountable. Given the catastrophic potential of biological weapons and the rapid pace of bio-technology development, the United States reserves the right to make any adjustment in the assurance that may be warranted by the evolution and proliferation of the biological weapons threat and U.S. capacities to counter that threat.

In the case of countries not covered by this assurance – states that possess nuclear weapons and states not in compliance with their nuclear non-proliferation obligations – there remains a narrow range of contingencies in which U.S. nuclear weapons may still play a role in deterring a conventional or CBW attack against the United States or its allies and partners. The United States is therefore not prepared at the present time to adopt a universal policy that deterring nuclear attack is the sole purpose of nuclear weapons, but will work to establish conditions under which such a policy could be safely adopted.

Yet that does not mean that our willingness to use nuclear weapons against countries not covered by the new assurance has in any way increased. Indeed, the United States wishes to stress that it would only consider the use of nuclear weapons in extreme circumstances to defend the vital interests of the United States or its allies and partners. It is in the U.S. interest and that of all other nations that the nearly 65-year record of nuclear non-use be extended forever.

Accordingly, among the key conclusions of the NPR:

- The United States will continue to strengthen conventional capabilities and reduce the role of nuclear weapons in deterring non-nuclear attacks, with the objective of making deterrence of nuclear attack on the United States or our allies and partners the sole purpose of U.S. nuclear weapons.

- The United States would only consider the use of nuclear weapons in extreme circumstances to defend the vital interests of the United States or its allies and partners.

- The United States will not use or threaten to use nuclear weapons against non-nuclear weapons states that are party to the NPT and in compliance with their nuclear non-proliferation obligations.

Maintaining Strategic Deterrence and Stability at Reduced Nuclear Force Levels

Since the end of the Cold War, the United States and Russia have reduced operationally deployed strategic nuclear weapons by about 75 percent, but both still retain many more nuclear weapons than they need for deterrence. The Administration is committed to working with Russia to preserve stability at significantly reduced force levels.

New START. The next step in this process is to replace the now-expired 1991 START I Treaty with another verifiable agreement, New START. An early task for the NPR was to develop U.S. positions for the New START negotiations and to consider how U.S. forces could be structured in light of the reductions required by the new agreement. The NPR reached the following conclusions:

- Stable deterrence can be maintained while reducing U.S. strategic delivery vehicles – intercontinental ballistic missiles (ICBMs), submarine-launched ballistic missiles (SLBMs), and nuclear-capable heavy bombers – by approximately 50 percent from the START I level, and reducing accountable strategic warheads by approximately 30 percent from the Moscow Treaty level.

- Building on NPR analysis, the United States agreed with Russia to New START limits of 1,550 accountable strategic warheads, 700 deployed strategic delivery vehicles, and a combined limit of 800 deployed and non-deployed strategic launchers.

- The U.S. nuclear Triad of ICBMs, SLBMs, and nuclear-capable heavy bombers will be maintained under New START.

- All U.S. ICBMs will be "de-MIRVed" to a single warhead each to increase stability.

- Contributions by non-nuclear systems to U.S. regional deterrence and reassurance goals will be preserved by avoiding limitations on missile defenses and preserving options for using heavy bombers and long-range missile systems in conventional roles.

Maximizing Presidential decision time. The NPR concluded that the current alert posture of U.S. strategic forces – with heavy bombers off full-time alert, nearly all ICBMs on alert, and a significant number of SSBNs at sea at any given time – should be maintained for the present. It also concluded that efforts should continue to diminish further the possibility of nuclear launches resulting from accidents, unauthorized actions, or misperceptions and to maximize the time available to the President to consider whether to authorize the use of nuclear weapons. Key steps include:

- Continuing the practice of "open-ocean targeting" of all ICBMs and SLBMs so that, in the highly unlikely event of an unauthorized or accidental launch, the missile would land in the open ocean, and asking Russia to re-confirm its commitment to this practice.

- Further strengthening the U.S. command and control system to maximize Presidential decision time in a nuclear crisis.

- Exploring new modes of ICBM basing that enhance survivability and further reduce any incentives for prompt launch.

Reinforcing strategic stability. Given that Russia and China are currently modernizing their nuclear capabilities – and that both are claiming U.S. missile defense and conventionally-armed missile programs are destabilizing – maintaining strategic stability with the two countries will be an important challenge in the years ahead.

- The United States will pursue high-level, bilateral dialogues on strategic stability with both Russia and China which are aimed at fostering more stable, resilient, and transparent strategic relationships.

A strategic dialogue with Russia will allow the United States to explain that our missile defenses and any future U.S. conventionally-armed long-range ballistic missile systems are designed to address newly emerging regional threats, and are not intended to affect the strategic balance with Russia. For its part, Russia could explain its modernization programs, clarify its current military doctrine (especially the extent to which it places importance on nuclear weapons), and discuss steps it could take to allay concerns in the West about its non-strategic nuclear arsenal, such as further consolidating its non-strategic systems in a small number of secure facilities deep within Russia.

With China, the purpose of a dialogue on strategic stability is to provide a venue and mechanism for each side to communicate its views about the other's strategies, policies, and programs on nuclear weapons and other strategic capabilities. The goal of such a dialogue is to enhance confidence, improve transparency, and reduce mistrust. As stated in the 2010 Ballistic Missile Defense Review Report, "maintaining strategic stability in the U.S.-China relationship is as important to this Administration as maintaining strategic stability with other major powers."

Future nuclear reductions. The President has directed a review of post-New START arms control objectives, to consider future reductions in nuclear weapons. Several factors will influence the magnitude and pace of future reductions in U.S. nuclear forces below New START levels.

First, any future nuclear reductions must continue to strengthen deterrence of potential regional adversaries, strategic stability vis-à-vis Russia and China, and assurance of our allies and partners. This will require an updated assessment of deterrence requirements; further improvements in U.S., allied, and partner non-nuclear capabilities; focused reductions in strategic and non-strategic weapons; and close consultations with allies and partners. The United States will continue to ensure that, in the calculations of any potential opponent, the perceived gains of attacking the United States or its allies and partners would be far outweighed by the unacceptable costs of the response.

Second, implementation of the Stockpile Stewardship Program and the nuclear infrastructure investments recommended in the NPR will allow the United States to shift away from retaining large numbers of non-deployed warheads as a hedge against technical or geopolitical surprise, allowing major reductions in the nuclear stockpile. These investments are essential to facilitating reductions while sustaining deterrence under New START and beyond.

Third, Russia's nuclear force will remain a significant factor in determining how much and how fast we are prepared to reduce U.S. forces. Because of our improved relations, the need for strict numerical parity between the two countries is no longer as compelling as it was during the Cold War. But large disparities in nuclear capabilities could raise concerns on both sides and among U.S. allies and partners, and may not be conducive to maintaining a stable, long-term strategic relationship, especially as nuclear forces are significantly reduced. Therefore, we will place importance on Russia joining us as we move to lower levels.

Key NPR recommendations include:

- Conduct follow-on analysis to set goals for future nuclear reductions below the levels expected in New START, while strengthening deterrence of potential regional adversaries, strategic stability vis-à-vis Russia and China, and assurance of our allies and partners.

- Address non-strategic nuclear weapons, together with the non-deployed nuclear weapons of both sides, in any post-New START negotiations with Russia.

- Implement U.S. nuclear force reductions in ways that maintain the reliability and effectiveness of security assurances to our allies and partners. The United States will consult with allies and partners in developing its approach to post-New START negotiations.

Strengthening Regional Deterrence and Reassuring U.S. Allies and Partners

The United States is fully committed to strengthening bilateral and regional security ties and working with allies and partners to adapt these relationships to 21st century challenges. Such security relationships are critical in deterring potential threats, and can also serve our non-proliferation goals – by demonstrating to neighboring states that their pursuit of nuclear weapons will only undermine their goal of achieving military or political advantages, and by reassuring non-nuclear U.S. allies and partners that their security interests can be protected without their own nuclear deterrent capabilities.

U.S. nuclear weapons have played an essential role in extending deterrence to U.S. allies and partners against nuclear attacks or nuclear-backed coercion by states in their region that possess or are seeking nuclear weapons. A credible U.S. "nuclear umbrella" has been provided by a combination of means – the strategic forces of the U.S. Triad, non-strategic nuclear weapons deployed forward in key regions, and U.S.-based nuclear weapons that could be deployed forward quickly to meet regional contingencies. The mix of deterrence means has varied over time and from region to region.

Defense Secretary Robert M. Gates conducts a press conference following the NATO Defense Ministerial in Istanbul, Turkey, Feb. 5, 2010. DoD photo by Cherie Cullen.

In Europe, forward-deployed U.S. nuclear weapons have been reduced dramatically since the end of the Cold War, but a small number of U.S. nuclear weapons remain. Although the risk of nuclear attack against NATO members is at an historic low, the presence of U.S. nuclear weapons – combined with NATO's unique nuclear sharing arrangements under which non-nuclear members participate in nuclear planning and possess specially configured aircraft capable of delivering nuclear weapons – contribute to Alliance cohesion and provide reassurance to allies and partners who feel exposed to regional threats. The role of nuclear weapons in defending Alliance members will be discussed this year in connection with NATO's revision of its Strategic Concept. Any changes in NATO's nuclear posture should only be taken after a thorough review within – and decision by – the Alliance.

In Asia and the Middle East – where there are no multilateral alliance structures analogous to NATO – the United States has maintained extended deterrence through bilateral alliances and security relationships and through its forward military presence and security guarantees. When the Cold War ended, the United States withdrew its forward deployed nuclear weapons from the Pacific region, including removing nuclear weapons from naval surface vessels and general purpose submarines. Since then, it has relied on its central strategic forces and the capacity to re-deploy nuclear systems in East Asia in times of crisis.

Although nuclear weapons have proved to be a key component of U.S. assurances to allies and partners, the United States has relied increasingly on non-nuclear elements to strengthen regional security architectures, including a forward U.S. conventional presence and effective theater ballistic missile defenses. As the role of nuclear weapons is reduced in U.S. national security strategy, these non-nuclear elements will take on a greater share of the deterrence burden. Moreover, an indispensable ingredient of effective regional deterrence is not only non-nuclear but also non-military – strong, trusting political relationships between the United States and its allies and partners.

Non-strategic nuclear weapons. The United States has reduced non-strategic (or "tactical") nuclear weapons dramatically since the end of the Cold War. Today, it keeps only a limited number of forward deployed nuclear weapons in Europe, plus a small number of nuclear weapons stored in the United States for possible overseas deployment in support of extended deterrence to allies and partners worldwide. Russia maintains a much larger force of non-strategic nuclear weapons, a significant number of which are deployed near the territories of several North Atlantic Treaty Organization (NATO) countries.

The NPR concluded that the United States will:

- Retain the capability to forward-deploy U.S. nuclear weapons on tactical fighter-bombers and heavy bombers, and proceed with full scope life extension for the B-61 bomb including enhancing safety, security, and use control.

- Retire the nuclear-equipped sea-launched cruise missile (TLAM-N).

- Continue to maintain and develop long-range strike capabilities that supplement U.S. forward military presence and strengthen regional deterrence.

- Continue and, where appropriate, expand consultations with allies and partners to address how to ensure the credibility and effectiveness of the U.S. extended deterrent. No changes in U.S. extended deterrence capabilities will be made without close consultations with our allies and partners.

Sustaining a Safe, Secure, and Effective Nuclear Arsenal

The United States is committed to ensuring that its nuclear weapons remain safe, secure, and effective. Since the end of U.S. nuclear testing in 1992, our nuclear warheads have been maintained and certified as safe and reliable through a Stockpile Stewardship Program that has extended the lives of warheads by refurbishing them to nearly original specifications. Looking ahead three decades, the NPR considered how best to extend the lives of existing nuclear warheads consistent with the congressionally mandated Stockpile Management Program and U.S. non-proliferation goals, and reached the following conclusions:

- The United States will not conduct nuclear testing and will pursue ratification and entry into force of the Comprehensive Nuclear Test Ban Treaty.

- The United States will not develop new nuclear warheads. Life Extension Programs (LEPs) will use only nuclear components based on previously tested designs, and will not support new military missions or provide for new military capabilities.

- The United States will study options for ensuring the safety, security, and reliability of nuclear warheads on a case-by-case basis, consistent with the congressionally mandated Stockpile Management Program. The full range of LEP approaches will be considered: refurbishment of existing warheads, reuse of nuclear components from different warheads, and replacement of nuclear components.

- In any decision to proceed to engineering development for warhead LEPs, the United States will give strong preference to options for refurbishment or reuse. Replacement of nuclear components would be undertaken only if critical Stockpile Management Program goals could not otherwise be met, and if specifically authorized by the President and approved by Congress.

Consistent with these conclusions, the NPR recommended:

- Funding fully the ongoing LEP for the W-76 submarine-based warhead and the LEP study and follow-on activities for the B-61 bomb; and

- Initiating a study of LEP options for the W-78 ICBM warhead, including the possibility of using the resulting warhead also on SLBMs to reduce the number of warhead types.

In order to remain safe, secure, and effective, the U.S. nuclear stockpile must be supported by a modern physical infrastructure – comprised of the national security laboratories and a complex of supporting facilities – and a highly capable workforce with the specialized skills needed to sustain the nuclear deterrent. As the United States reduces the numbers of nuclear weapons, the reliability of the remaining weapons in the stockpile – and the quality of the facilities needed to sustain it – become more important.

Human capital is also a concern. The national security laboratories have found it increasingly difficult to attract and retain the most promising scientists and engineers of the next generation. The Administration's commitment to a clear, long-term plan for managing the stockpile, as well as to preventing proliferation and nuclear terrorism will enhance recruitment and retention of the scientists and engineers of tomorrow, by providing the opportunity to engage in challenging and meaningful research and development activities.

The NPR concluded:

- The science, technology and engineering base, vital for stockpile stewardship as well as providing insights for non-proliferation, must be strengthened.

- Increased investments in the nuclear weapons complex of facilities and personnel are required to ensure the long-term safety, security, and effectiveness of our nuclear arsenal. New facilities will be sized to support the requirements of the stockpile stewardship and management plan being developed by the National Nuclear Security Administration.

- Increased funding is needed for the Chemistry and Metallurgy Research Replacement Project at Los Alamos National Laboratory to replace the existing 50-year old facility, and to develop a new Uranium Processing Facility at the Y-12 Plant in Oak Ridge, Tennessee.

Looking Ahead: Toward a World without Nuclear Weapons

Pursuing the recommendations of the 2010 Nuclear Posture Review will strengthen the security of the United States and its allies and partners and bring us significant steps closer to the President's vision of a world without nuclear weapons.

The conditions that would ultimately permit the United States and others to give up their nuclear weapons without risking greater international instability and insecurity are very demanding. Among those conditions are success in halting the proliferation of nuclear weapons, much greater transparency into the programs and capabilities of key countries of concern, verification methods and technologies capable of detecting violations of disarmament obligations, enforcement measures strong and credible enough to deter such violations, and ultimately the resolution of regional disputes that can motivate rival states to acquire and maintain nuclear weapons. Clearly, such conditions do not exist today.

But we can – and must – work actively to create those conditions. We can take the practical steps identified in the 2010 NPR that will not only move us toward the ultimate goal of eliminating all nuclear weapons worldwide but will, in their own right, reinvigorate the global nuclear non-proliferation regime, erect higher barriers to the acquisition of nuclear weapons and nuclear materials by terrorist groups, and strengthen U.S. and international security.

INTRODUCTION

A year ago in Prague, President Obama offered a new direction for coping with 21st century nuclear dangers, declaring that to overcome grave and growing threats of nuclear terrorism and nuclear proliferation, the United States will "seek the peace and security of a world without nuclear weapons." He recognized that such an ambitious goal could not be reached quickly – perhaps, he said, not in his lifetime. But the President expressed his determination to take concrete steps toward that goal, including by reducing U.S. nuclear weapons and their role in U.S. national security strategy. At the same time, he pledged that as long as nuclear weapons exist, the United States will maintain a safe, secure, and effective arsenal, both to deter potential adversaries and to assure U.S. allies and other security partners that they can count on America's security commitments.

This Nuclear Posture Review (NPR) report outlines the Administration's approach to promoting the President's agenda for reducing nuclear dangers and pursuing the goal of a world without nuclear weapons – while simultaneously advancing broader U.S. security interests, consistent with the President's national security priorities and the supporting defense strategy objectives identified in the 2010 Quadrennial Defense Review. The 2010 NPR represents the third comprehensive assessment of U.S. nuclear policy and strategy conducted by the United States since the end of the Cold War. Previous reviews were completed in 1994 and 2001.

As mandated by Congress, the 2010 NPR was conducted by the Secretary of Defense in consultation with the Secretaries of State and Energy. Within the Department of Defense, the review was led jointly by the Office of the Secretary of Defense and the Joint Staff. The Military Departments and Combatant Commands also contributed to the analytical work; there was especially close collaboration with U.S. Strategic Command. Because of the breadth of issues addressed, the review involved a number of additional departments and agencies, including the Departments of Homeland Security and Treasury, and the Office of the Director of National Intelligence. The review also benefited from extensive consultations with Congress, U.S. allies, and other interested stakeholders. The National Security Council and its supporting interagency bodies met throughout the review to consider key issues of strategy and policy.

In Presidential guidance initiating the NPR, the President called for a thorough review of U.S. nuclear weapons policies and force posture. He directed that the review bring forward options for discussion aimed at multiple objectives: reducing the role and numbers of U.S. nuclear weapons; strengthening deterrence of adversaries; reassuring allies and partners, who depend on the U.S. commitment to extended deterrence; enhancing strategic stability; and moving demonstrably toward the ultimate goal of the elimination of nuclear weapons.

INTRODUCTION

A key premise of the 2010 NPR was that any successful strategy for achieving these objectives must be *balanced*, with movement in one area enabling and reinforcing progress in other areas. For example, increased infrastructure investment and a sound Stockpile Stewardship Program will facilitate reductions in both deployed and non-deployed nuclear weapons. The elements of such a strategy must also be *integrated*, both nationally – across federal agencies and between the executive and legislative branches – and internationally among a wide range of partner governments. And an effective strategy must be *sustained* over time, with support from a long succession of U.S. Administrations and Congresses. A balanced, integrated, and sustained strategy will require a strong bipartisan consensus. Forging such a consensus is a central purpose of this NPR.

After describing fundamental changes in the international security environment and U.S. adjustments to date, the NPR report focuses on five key objectives of our nuclear weapons policies and posture:

1. Preventing nuclear proliferation and nuclear terrorism;

2. Reducing the role of U.S. nuclear weapons in U.S. national security strategy;

3. Maintaining strategic deterrence and stability at lower nuclear force levels;

4. Strengthening regional deterrence and reassuring U.S. allies and partners; and

5. Sustaining a safe, secure, and effective nuclear arsenal.

A final section of the NPR considers the path ahead for U.S. nuclear strategy and posture over the coming years and decades.

THE CHANGED – AND CHANGING – NUCLEAR SECURITY ENVIRONMENT

The international security environment has changed dramatically since the end of the Cold War. The threat of global nuclear war has become remote, but the risk of nuclear attack has increased.

The Threat of Nuclear Proliferation and Nuclear Terrorism

The most immediate and extreme threat today is nuclear terrorism. Al Qaeda and their extremist allies are seeking nuclear weapons. We must assume they would use such weapons if they managed to obtain them. Although terrorist groups are currently believed to lack the resources to produce weapons-usable nuclear material themselves, the vulnerability to theft or seizure of vast stocks of such nuclear materials around the world, and the availability of sensitive equipment and technologies in the nuclear black market, create a serious risk that terrorists may acquire what they need to build a nuclear weapon.

To date, the international community has made progress toward achieving a global "lock down" of nuclear weapons, materials, and associated technology, but much more work needs to be done. In addition, the United States and the international community have improving but currently insufficient capabilities to detect, interdict, and defeat efforts to covertly deliver nuclear materials or weapons—and if an attack occurs, to respond to minimize casualties and economic impact as well as to attribute the source of the attack and take strong action.

Today's other pressing threat is nuclear proliferation. Additional countries – especially those at odds with the United States, its allies and partners, and the broader international community – may acquire nuclear weapons. In pursuit of their nuclear ambitions, North Korea and Iran have violated non-proliferation obligations, defied directives of the United Nations Security Council, pursued missile delivery capabilities, and resisted international efforts to resolve through diplomatic means the crises

President Barack Obama chairs a United Nations Security Council meeting at UN Headquarters in New York, N.Y., Sept. 24, 2009. Official White House photo by Pete Souza.

they have created. Their illicit supply of arms and sensitive material and technologies has heightened global proliferation risks and regional tensions. Their provocative behavior has increased instability in their regions. Continued non-compliance with non-proliferation norms by these and other countries would seriously weaken the Nuclear Non-Proliferation Treaty (NPT), with adverse security implications for the United States and the international community at large.

The potential for regional aggression by these states raises challenges not only of deterrence, but also of reassuring U.S. allies and partners. In the Cold War, our allies sought assurance that they would remain safe in the face of Soviet threats because the United States was demonstrably committed to their security. Today's environment is quite different. Some U.S. allies are increasingly anxious about changes in the security environment, including nuclear and missile proliferation, and desire reassurance that the United States will remain committed to their security. A failure of reassurance could lead to a decision by one or more non-nuclear states to seek nuclear deterrents of their own, an outcome which could contribute to an unraveling of the NPT regime and to a greater likelihood of nuclear weapon use.

Despite these challenges, the NPT remains a cornerstone of the non-proliferation regime and has served the international community well over the past four decades. Its fundamental bargain is still sound: all parties have a right to peaceful nuclear power; states without nuclear weapons forsake them; and those with nuclear weapons work towards disarmament. However, with clear evidence of non-compliance with the NPT, the non-proliferation regime urgently requires strengthening.

Further, the International Atomic Energy Agency (IAEA), the international body charged with applying safeguards to ensure that nuclear facilities and materials are used only for peaceful purposes, currently lacks sufficient resources and authorities necessary to carry out its mission effectively.

Strategic Stability with Russia and China

While facing the urgent threats of nuclear terrorism and nuclear proliferation, the United States must continue to address the more familiar challenge of ensuring strategic stability with existing nuclear powers – most notably Russia and China. Russia remains America's only peer in the area of nuclear weapons capabilities. But the nature of the U.S.-Russia strategic and political relationship has changed fundamentally since the days of the Cold War. Policy differences continue to arise between the two countries, and Russia continues to modernize its still-formidable nuclear forces. But Russia and the United States have increased their cooperation in areas of shared interest, including preventing nuclear proliferation and nuclear terrorism. And the prospects for military confrontation have declined dramatically in recent decades.

While the United States and Russia have reduced deployed nuclear weapons by about 75 percent since the end of the Cold War, each still retains more nuclear weapons than necessary for stable deterrence. As the United States and Russia reduce their deployed strategic nuclear weapons and delivery vehicles under the New Strategic Arms Reduction Treaty (New START) and a follow-on agreement to it, maintaining a stable bilateral balance and avoiding dangerous nuclear competition will be key objectives.

The United States and China are increasingly interdependent and their shared responsibilities for addressing global security threats, such as WMD proliferation and terrorism, are growing. The United States welcomes a strong, prosperous, and successful China that plays a greater global role in supporting international rules, norms, and institutions.

At the same time, the United States and China's Asian neighbors remain concerned about the pace and scope of China's current military modernization efforts, including its quantitative and qualitative modernization of its nuclear capabilities. China's nuclear arsenal remains much smaller than the arsenals of Russia and the United States. But the lack of transparency surrounding its programs – their pace and scope as well as the strategy and doctrine guiding them – raises questions about China's future strategic intentions.

Adapting to a Changed Security Environment

These changes in the nuclear threat environment – especially the heightened concern about nuclear terrorism and nuclear proliferation and the less dangerous strategic interaction between the United States and Russia – have not emerged overnight. They have developed over the last twenty years, and Administrations of both parties have responded with modifications of U.S. nuclear weapons policies and force posture. But those modifications have not gone far or fast enough. As the President has said, we have to "put an end to Cold War thinking."

- The United States has begun to shift our focus to the dangers of nuclear proliferation and nuclear terrorism, but we need to intensify our efforts to build broad international support for the rigorous measures needed to prevent these dangers.

- The United States has sought to prevent the emergence of new regional nuclear-armed states, but we need to do more to enhance regional security architectures to reassure our allies and partners that our commitments to their defense will remain strong and reliable.

- The United States and Russia have deeply reduced their nuclear forces from Cold War levels, but both still retain many more nuclear weapons than needed.

- The United States has reduced our reliance on nuclear weapons as Cold War nuclear rivalries have eased and as our conventional military forces and missile defense capabilities have strengthened, but we have sent mixed signals about the importance we place on nuclear weapons in our national security strategy.

- The United States has maintained a safe, secure, and effective nuclear stockpile without nuclear testing since 1992, but significant investments are needed in both physical and human capital to ensure that the stockpile can be maintained without ever needing to test again.

The growing dangers of nuclear proliferation and nuclear terrorism have altered the hierarchy of our nuclear concerns and strategic objectives. In coming years, we must give top priority to discouraging additional countries from acquiring nuclear weapons capabilities and stopping terrorist groups from acquiring the materials to build nuclear bombs. At the same time, we must continue to maintain stable strategic relationships with Russia and China and counter threats posed by any emerging nuclear-armed states, thereby protecting the United States and our allies and partners against nuclear threats or intimidation, and reducing any incentives our non-nuclear allies and partners might have to seek their own nuclear deterrents.

Implications for U.S. Nuclear Weapons Policies and Force Structure

The massive nuclear arsenal we inherited from the Cold War era of bipolar military confrontation is poorly suited to address the challenges posed by suicidal terrorists and unfriendly regimes seeking nuclear weapons. Therefore, it is essential that we better align our nuclear policies and posture to our most urgent priorities – preventing nuclear terrorism and nuclear proliferation.

This does not mean that our nuclear deterrent has become irrelevant. Indeed, as long as nuclear weapons exist, the United States will maintain safe, secure, and effective nuclear forces, including deployed and stockpiled nuclear weapons, highly capable nuclear delivery systems and command and control capabilities, and the physical infrastructure and the expert personnel needed to sustain them. These nuclear forces will continue to play an essential role in deterring potential adversaries, reassuring allies and partners around the world, and promoting stability globally and in key regions.

But fundamental changes in the international security environment in recent years – including the growth of unrivaled U.S. conventional military capabilities, major improvements in missile defenses, and the easing of Cold War rivalries – enable us to fulfill those objectives at significantly lower nuclear force levels and with reduced reliance on nuclear weapons. Therefore, without jeopardizing our traditional deterrence and reassurance goals, we are now able to shape our nuclear weapons policies and force structure in ways that will better enable us to meet today's most pressing security challenges.

- By reducing the role and numbers of U.S. nuclear weapons – and thereby demonstrating that we are meeting our NPT Article VI obligation to make progress toward nuclear disarmament – we can put ourselves in a much stronger position to persuade our NPT partners to join with us in adopting the measures needed to reinvigorate the non-proliferation regime and secure nuclear materials worldwide against theft or seizure by terrorist groups.

- By maintaining a credible nuclear deterrent and reinforcing regional security architectures with missile defenses and other conventional military capabilities, we can reassure our non-nuclear allies and partners worldwide of our security commitments to them and confirm that they do not need nuclear weapons capabilities of their own.

- By pursuing a sound Stockpile Management Program for extending the life of U.S. nuclear weapons, we can ensure a safe, secure, and effective deterrent without the development of new nuclear warheads or further nuclear testing.

- By modernizing our aging nuclear weapons-supporting facilities and investing in human capital, we can substantially reduce the number of stockpiled nuclear weapons we retain as a hedge against technical or geopolitical surprise, accelerate the dismantlement of nuclear weapons no longer required for our deterrent, and improve our understanding of foreign nuclear weapons activities.

Vice President Joseph R. Biden delivers a speech on nuclear security and implementing the President's Prague agenda before Secretary of Defense Robert Gates, Secretary of Energy Steven Chu, Vice Chairman of the Joint Chiefs of Staff General James Cartwright, and several hundred guests, at the National Defense University on Feb. 18, 2010. National Defense University photo.

- By promoting strategic stability with Russia and China and improving transparency and mutual confidence, we can help create the conditions for moving toward a world without nuclear weapons and build a stronger basis for addressing the threats of nuclear proliferation and nuclear terrorism.

- By working to reduce the salience of nuclear weapons in international affairs and moving step-by-step toward eliminating them, we can reverse the growing expectation that we are destined to live in a world with many nuclear-armed states, and decrease incentives for additional countries to hedge against an uncertain and dangerous future by pursuing nuclear options of their own. Creating these conditions will reduce the likelihood of nuclear weapon use.

In sum, the security environment has changed in fundamental ways since the end of the Cold War. The landscape of threats and challenges has evolved. But a changing landscape has also brought with it some valuable new opportunities. Accordingly, U.S. policy priorities must shift. The U.S. policy agenda must reflect a clear and current understanding of how U.S. nuclear strategy and posture shape these international dynamics.

PREVENTING NUCLEAR PROLIFERATION AND NUCLEAR TERRORISM

As part of our effort to move toward a world free of nuclear weapons, the United States will lead expanded international efforts to rebuild and strengthen the global nuclear non-proliferation regime and to accelerate efforts to prevent nuclear terrorism. Concerns have grown in recent years that unless today's dangerous trends are arrested and reversed, before long we will be living in a world with a steadily growing number of nuclear-armed states and an increasing likelihood of terrorists getting their hands on nuclear weapons. Therefore, for the first time, the 2010 NPR places this priority atop the U.S. nuclear agenda.

The United States is committed to renewing and strengthening the Nuclear Non-Proliferation Treaty (NPT) and the global nuclear non-proliferation regime it anchors to cope with the challenges of non-compliance and of the growth of nuclear power. We support expanding access to the benefits of peaceful nuclear technology, but this must be done in a way that does not promote proliferation of nuclear weapons capabilities. To strengthen the regime, the United States seeks to champion and reaffirm through its own actions the grand bargain that underpins the treaty: states without nuclear weapons will not acquire them, states with nuclear weapons will move toward disarmament, and all Parties can have access to peaceful nuclear energy under effective verification.

As part of this effort, the United States seeks to bolster the nuclear non-proliferation regime by:

- Reversing the nuclear ambitions of North Korea and Iran. We have demonstrated that we are prepared to engage multilaterally and bilaterally with these states to arrive at negotiated solutions that provide for their political and economic integration with the international community, while verifiably confirming they are not pursuing nuclear weapons capabilities. However, their continued defiance of international norms and agreements will lead only to their further isolation and increasing international pressure.

- Strengthening International Atomic Energy Agency (IAEA) safeguards. NPT Members, particularly non-nuclear weapons states, rely for security on assurances that countries will not divert nuclear material to illicit nuclear weapons programs. IAEA safeguards are essential in maintaining that assurance. To deter and detect safeguards violations, the IAEA must be given additional financial resources and verification authorities, and all countries should adhere to the IAEA Additional Protocol. The United States is committed to expanding financial support for the regular IAEA budget and will continue to push for stronger institutional support from other states, while we continue to increase our own extra-budgetary contributions. The U.S. Next Generation Safeguards Initiative will assist the IAEA to confront new challenges far into the future by helping develop the tools, authorities, capabilities, technologies, expertise, and resources needed to meet current and future safeguard challenges.

- Creating consequences for non-compliance. It is not enough to detect non-compliance; violators must know that they will face consequences when they are caught. Moreover, states that violate their obligations must not be able to escape the consequences of their non-compliance by withdrawing from the NPT.

- Impeding sensitive nuclear trade. National and multilateral export and border controls must be strengthened, financial and other tools must be used to disrupt illicit proliferation networks, and tighter restrictions must be placed on the transfer of dual-use enrichment and reprocessing technologies. The United States has increased its funding to help countries improve strategic trade controls and improve targeting and inspection at border crossings. We also support development of a United Nations Security Council Resolution 1540 "trust fund" to assist countries in meeting their obligations under the resolution, including developing and enforcing national export controls to prevent non-state actors from obtaining weapons of mass destruction (WMD)-related materials and technology. We are implementing President Obama's pledge to make the Proliferation Security Initiative into a durable international institution, under which over 90 countries coordinate, share intelligence, and build capacity to interdict WMD-related transfers. And the United States is working to detect and disrupt the financing of nuclear proliferation and terrorism by identifying and prosecuting its networks and establishing international standards and best practices.

- Promoting the peaceful uses of nuclear energy without increasing proliferation risks. President Obama has called for the development of a new framework for international nuclear energy cooperation, which the United States is pursuing with the international community through the Global Nuclear Energy Partnership, which includes 25 partner and 31 observer nations. To reduce incentives for countries to pursue indigenous fuel cycle facilities, this new framework should include international fuel banks, such as the Russian Angarsk fuel bank approved by the IAEA in February 2010, multilateral fuel-supply assurances, agreements by suppliers to take back spent fuel, and spent fuel repositories. Cradle-to-grave nuclear fuel management could be one important element of this new framework. The United States will also continue to assist other countries in benefitting from the other peaceful applications of nuclear materials, including for medical and agricultural uses and pure research.

The United States is committed to improving nuclear security worldwide in order to prevent nuclear terrorism. This cannot be accomplished by the United States alone. All states have a fundamental responsibility to ensure the security and control of nuclear materials and weapons in their possession. Further, this ambitious agenda requires the active engagement of a broad coalition of nations acting in concert. The United States has given high priority to strengthening and accelerating international efforts to prevent nuclear terrorism by:

- Pursuing aggressively the President's Prague initiative, endorsed in United Nations Security Council Resolution 1887, to secure all vulnerable nuclear materials worldwide. The United States will be doing so by expanding our cooperation with other countries and strengthening nuclear security standards, practices, and international safeguards.

- Hosting the April 2010 Nuclear Security Summit, where leaders of over 40 countries will commit to fight nuclear smuggling and terrorism and put in place effective nuclear security measures.

- Increasing funding in fiscal year (FY) 2011 for the National Nuclear Security Administration's nuclear non-proliferation programs to $2.7 billion, an increase of more than 25 percent.

In May 2009, the National Nuclear Security Administration (NNSA) announced the removal of 73.7 kilograms (162.5 pounds) of Russian-origin highly enriched uranium (HEU) "spent" nuclear fuel from Kazakhstan. The material was removed and returned to Russia for storage at a secure nuclear facility in a series of four shipments between December 2008 and May 2009. NNSA photo.

- Accelerating the Global Threat Reduction Initiative to remove and secure high-priority vulnerable nuclear material around the world, convert additional research reactors to operate on fuel that cannot be used in nuclear weapons, and complete the repatriation of U.S.- and Russian-origin highly enriched uranium from research reactors worldwide.

- Accelerating the International Nuclear Material Protection and Cooperation Program to install nuclear security upgrades at Russian weapons complex sites and to expand cooperation to new priority countries beyond Russia and the former Soviet Union.

- Securing and eliminating weapons of mass destruction and their means of delivery through cooperative threat reduction programs at the Departments of Defense, State, and Energy, including the flagship Nunn-Lugar program. And assisting other countries to strengthen their national capacities for nuclear materials protection, control, and accounting through these programs, United Nations Security Council Resolution 1540, and multilateral cooperative threat reduction programs.

- Enhancing national and international capabilities to detect and interdict smuggled nuclear materials. We are expanding the Container Security Initiative to screen U.S.-bound cargo and the Second Line of Defense and Megaports programs to install radiation detectors at key borders, airports, and seaports. We also are making the 77-country Global Initiative to Combat Nuclear Terrorism a durable international institution. The Initiative coordinates expertise, shares information, and integrates capabilities to deter, detect, interdict, mitigate, and respond to acts of nuclear terrorism.

- Continue to strengthen our nuclear forensics efforts to improve the ability to identify the source of nuclear material used or intended for use in a terrorist nuclear explosive device.

- Renewing the U.S. commitment to hold fully accountable any state, terrorist group, or other non-state actor that supports or enables terrorist efforts to obtain or use weapons of mass destruction, whether by facilitating, financing, or providing expertise or safe haven for such efforts.

U.S. arms control and disarmament efforts, as well as other means of reducing the role of nuclear weapons and moving toward a world without them, can make a major contribution to our goal of preventing nuclear proliferation and nuclear terrorism. By demonstrating that we take seriously our NPT obligation to pursue nuclear disarmament, we strengthen our ability to mobilize broad international support for the measures needed to reinforce the non-proliferation regime and secure nuclear materials worldwide. We are doing so by:

- Concluding a verifiable New Strategic Arms Reduction Treaty (New START) that limits U.S. and Russian nuclear forces to levels well below those provided for in the 1991 START Treaty and the 2002 Moscow Treaty. U.S. ratification and subsequent implementation of the new Treaty will be a concrete step on the path to nuclear disarmament. The verification and transparency measures included in the Treaty will help ensure stability and predictability in the U.S.-Russia strategic relationship. Implementation of the treaty also will set the stage for deeper, verifiable nuclear reductions. As the United States and Russia reduce their deployed weapons through New START, the United States will pursue negotiations for deeper reductions and greater transparency in partnership with Russia. Over time, we will also engage with other nuclear weapon states, including China, on ways to expand the nuclear reduction process in the future. This process should include efforts to improve transparency of states' nuclear policies, strategies, and programs.

- Pursuing ratification and early entry into force of the Comprehensive Nuclear Test Ban Treaty (CTBT). Ratification of the CTBT is central to leading other nuclear weapons states toward a world of diminished reliance on nuclear weapons, reduced nuclear competition, and eventual nuclear disarmament. U.S. ratification could also encourage ratification by other states, including China, and provide incentives for the remaining states to work toward entry into force of the treaty. Further, U.S. ratification of the CTBT would enable us to encourage non-NPT Parties to follow the lead of the NPT-recognized Nuclear Weapon States in formalizing a heretofore voluntary testing moratorium, and thus strengthen strategic stability by reducing the salience of nuclear weapons in those states' national defense strategies.

- Seeking commencement of negotiations on a verifiable Fissile Material Cutoff Treaty (FMCT) to halt the production of fissile material for use in nuclear weapons. Given that some states continue to produce fissile materials for nuclear weapons, a multilateral, binding FMCT is needed to provide a quantitative cap on the potential growth of existing nuclear weapons stockpiles. As a result, the United States is committed to prompt negotiation of an FMCT with appropriate monitoring and verification provisions. The United States recognizes that such negotiations will be complex and will take time; however, a carefully crafted and verifiable FMCT will enhance our national security and contribute to nuclear stability worldwide.

- Working with the Russian Federation to jointly eliminate 68 tons of weapons-grade plutonium no longer needed for defense purposes.

- Initiating a comprehensive national research and development program to support continued progress toward a world free of nuclear weapons, including expanded work on verification technologies and the development of transparency measures. Such technologies will help us manage risk as we continue down this path by ensuring that we are able to detect potential clandestine weapons programs, foreign nuclear materials, and weapons production facilities and processes.

A Nuclear Forensics Ground Collection Team in protection equipment screens a debris sample in a field exercise in Idaho. Defense Threat Reduction Agency photo.

REDUCING THE ROLE OF U.S. NUCLEAR WEAPONS

The role of nuclear weapons in U.S. national security and U.S. military strategy has been reduced significantly in recent decades, but further steps can and should be taken at this time.

The fundamental role of U.S. nuclear weapons, which will continue as long as nuclear weapons exist, is to deter nuclear attack on the United States, our allies, and partners.

During the Cold War, the United States also reserved the right to use nuclear weapons in response to a massive conventional attack by the Soviet Union and its Warsaw Pact allies. Moreover, after the United States gave up its own chemical and biological weapons (CBW) pursuant to international treaties (while some states continued to possess or pursue them) the United States reserved the right to employ nuclear weapons to deter CBW attack on the United States and its allies and partners.

Since the end of the Cold War, the strategic situation has changed in fundamental ways.

First, and foremost, the Soviet Union and the Warsaw Pact are gone. Russia is not an enemy, and is increasingly a partner in confronting proliferation and other emerging threats. And all of the non-Soviet former members of the Warsaw Pact are now members of the North Atlantic Treaty Organization (NATO).

Second, U.S., allied, and partner conventional military capabilities now provide a wide range of effective conventional response options to deter and if necessary defeat conventional threats from regional actors. Major improvements in missile defenses and counter-weapons of mass destruction (WMD) capabilities have strengthened deterrence and defense against CBW attack.

Given these developments, the role of U.S. nuclear weapons to deter and respond to non-nuclear attacks—conventional, biological, or chemical—has declined significantly. The United States will continue to reduce the role of nuclear weapons in deterring non-nuclear attack.

To that end, the United States is now prepared to strengthen its long-standing "negative security assurance" by declaring that the United States will not use or threaten to use nuclear weapons against non-nuclear weapons states that are party to the Nuclear Non-Proliferation Treaty (NPT) and in compliance with their nuclear non-proliferation obligations.

This revised assurance is intended to underscore the security benefits of adhering to and fully complying with the NPT and persuade non-nuclear weapon states party to the Treaty to work with the United States and other interested parties to adopt effective measures to strengthen the non-proliferation regime.

In making this strengthened assurance, the United States affirms that any state eligible for the assurance that uses CBW against the United States or its allies and partners would face the prospect of a devastating conventional military response—and that any individuals responsible for the attack, whether national leaders or military commanders, would be held fully accountable. Given the catastrophic potential of biological weapons and the rapid pace of bio-technology development, the United States reserves the right to make any adjustment in the assurance that may be warranted by the evolution and proliferation of the biological weapons threat and U.S. capacities to counter that threat.

In the case of countries not covered by this assurance – states that possess nuclear weapons and states not in compliance with their nuclear non-proliferation obligations – there remains a narrow range of contingencies in which U.S. nuclear weapons may still play a role in deterring a conventional or CBW attack against the United States or its allies and partners. The United States is therefore not prepared at the present time to adopt a universal policy that the "sole purpose" of U.S. nuclear weapons is to deter nuclear attack on the United States and our allies and partners, but will work to establish conditions under which such a policy could be safely adopted.

A medium-range ballistic missile with a separating target is launched from the Pacific Missile Range Facility on Jun. 22, 2007 (left photo). Minutes later, a Standard Missile (SM-3) was launched from the Aegis combat system equipped Arleigh Burke class destroyer USS Decatur (DDG 73), successfully intercepting the ballistic missile threat target (right photo). It was the first time such a test was conducted from a ballistic missile defense equipped-U.S. Navy destroyer. U.S. Navy photos.

Yet this does not mean that our willingness to use nuclear weapons against countries not covered by the new assurance has in any way increased. Indeed, the United States wishes to stress that it would only consider the use of nuclear weapons in extreme circumstances to defend the vital interests of the United States or its allies and partners.

It is in the U.S. interest and that of all other nations that the nearly 65-year record of nuclear non-use be extended forever. As President Ronald Reagan declared, "A nuclear war cannot be won and must never be fought."

In summary, the following principles will guide U.S. nuclear policies:

- The United States will meet its commitment under Article VI of the NPT to pursue nuclear disarmament and will make demonstrable progress over the next five to ten years.

We will work to reduce the role and numbers of U.S. nuclear weapons while enhancing security for ourselves, and our allies and partners.

- The United States will continue to strengthen conventional capabilities and reduce the role of nuclear weapons in deterring non-nuclear attacks, with the objective of making deterrence of nuclear attack on the United States or our allies and partners the sole purpose of U.S. nuclear weapons.

- The United States would only consider the use of nuclear weapons in extreme circumstances to defend the vital interests of the United States or its allies and partners.

- The United States will not use or threaten to use nuclear weapons against non-nuclear weapons states that are party to the NPT and in compliance with their nuclear non-proliferation obligations.

MAINTAINING STRATEGIC DETERRENCE AND STABILITY AT REDUCED NUCLEAR FORCE LEVELS

Since the end of the Cold War, the United States and Russia have reduced operationally deployed strategic nuclear weapons by approximately 75 percent, but both still retain many more nuclear weapons than needed for deterrence. As an initial step, the Administration is committed to working with Russia to preserve stability at significantly reduced nuclear force levels, through the New Strategic Arms Reduction Treaty (New START).

Beyond New START's bilateral reductions in operationally deployed strategic forces, the NPR examined ways to minimize potential nuclear instability by maximizing the decision time provided to the President. Analysis also focused on our limited non-strategic nuclear weapons posture. Moreover, in our commitment to the long-term goal of a world without nuclear weapons, the NPR examined the full range of factors that will allow deeper reductions in U.S. nuclear force levels.

It is also clear that maintaining strategic stability at reduced force levels will be an enduring and evolving challenge for the United States in the years ahead. Ongoing nuclear and other military modernization efforts by Russia and China compound this challenge, making the need for strategic stability dialogues all the more critical.

Toward New START

U.S. strategic forces – comprised of submarine-launched ballistic missiles (SLBMs), inter-continental ballistic missiles (ICBMs), and nuclear-capable heavy bombers – continue to underwrite deterrence of nuclear attack against the United States, our allies, and partners.

Secretary of State Hillary Rodham Clinton meets with Russian President Dmitry Medvedev and Russian Foreign Minister Sergey Lavrov in Moscow, Russia, Oct. 13, 2009. State Department photo.

In the two decades since the end of the Cold War, the United States has reduced deployed warheads on strategic delivery systems by approximately 75 percent. The next step in this process is to replace the expired 1991 START I Treaty with another verifiable agreement, New START. U.S. and Russian negotiators have recently completed this agreement.

An early task of the NPR was to develop U.S. positions for the New START negotiations. In so doing, the review explored how a range of force structures might affect strategic stability at lower numbers. Further the NPR considered whether the nuclear Triad of SLBMs, ICBMs, and heavy bombers should be retained, and, if so, the necessary investments to sustain each Triad leg.

Determining New START Positions

Detailed NPR analysis of potential reductions in strategic weapons, conducted in spring 2009, concluded that the United States could sustain stable deterrence with significantly fewer deployed strategic nuclear warheads, assuming parallel Russian reductions. The NPR analysis considered several specific levels of nuclear weapons, all below current levels of approximately 2,200 deployed strategic warheads. Its conclusions, approved by the President, the Secretary of Defense, the Joint Chiefs of Staff, and Commander, U.S. Strategic Command, formed the basis for U.S. negotiations with Russia on New START. Because New START is intended to be only an initial step in a continuing process of bilateral nuclear reductions, this initial analysis used conservative assumptions to determine acceptable reductions in deployed strategic nuclear weapons.

New START will result in significant mutual limits in deployed strategic nuclear warheads, well below the 2,200 allowed under the Strategic Offensive Reductions Treaty (SORT), also known as the Moscow Treaty, which expires in 2012.

The NPR conducted detailed analysis to determine an appropriate limit on nuclear warheads and strategic delivery vehicles (SDVs). After determining that the United States should retain a nuclear Triad under New START, the NPR went on to assess the appropriate force structure for each Triad leg, namely the required numbers of strategic nuclear submarines (SSBNs) and SLBMs, ICBMs, and nuclear-capable heavy bombers. Analysis focused on meeting four requirements:

- Supporting strategic stability through an assured second-strike capability;

- Retaining sufficient force structure in each leg to allow the ability to hedge effectively by shifting weight from one Triad leg to another if necessary due to unexpected technological problems or operational vulnerabilities;

- Retaining a margin above the minimum required nuclear force structure for the possible addition of non-nuclear prompt-global strike capabilities (conventionally-armed ICBMs or SLBMs) that would be accountable under the Treaty; and

- Maintaining the needed capabilities over the next several decades or more, including retaining a sufficient cadre of trained military and civilian personnel and adequate infrastructure.

The 1991 START I, which expired in December 2009, limited the United States and Russia to 1600 SDVs each. While the United States has approximately 1,200 SDVs still accountable under the now-expired Treaty's counting rules, fewer than 900 are associated with deployed strategic nuclear weapons. The remainder are essentially "phantoms:" either conventional-only delivery systems, particularly B-1B bombers and SSGN submarines (converted from SSBNs to carry conventional sea-launched cruise missiles), or ICBM silos and heavy bombers that are no longer in use but which have not yet been eliminated.

The Secretary of Defense, the Joint Chiefs of Staff, and the Commander of U.S. Strategic Command supported reductions in limits on deployed as well as non-deployed U.S. SDVs. This recommendation was conditional on the exclusion of conventional B-1B bombers and U.S. SSGN submarines from accountability under the Treaty and the acceptance of the potential conversion of a subset of the B-52 fleet to a conventional-only capability.

Building on NPR analysis, the United States and Russia have agreed to mutual limits under the New START:

- A limit of 1,550 accountable strategic warheads;

- A separate limit of 700 deployed ICBMs, deployed SLBMs, and deployed nuclear-capable heavy bombers; and

- A combined limit of 800 deployed and non-deployed ICBM launchers, SLBM launchers, and nuclear capable heavy bombers.

Under the New START, dual-capable bombers will count as both one strategic delivery vehicle, and as one warhead. This counting rule was adopted in recognition of the facts that heavy bombers do not pose a first-strike threat to either side, and that on a day-to-day basis few or no bombers are loaded with nuclear weapons.

The Future of the Triad

After considering a wide range of possible options for the U.S. strategic nuclear posture, including some that involved eliminating a leg of the Triad, the NPR concluded that for planned reductions under New START, the United States should retain a smaller Triad of SLBMs, ICBMs, and heavy bombers. Retaining all three Triad legs will best maintain strategic stability at reasonable cost, while hedging against potential technical problems or vulnerabilities.

Air Force Global Strike Command officials assumed responsibility for the Air Force's nuclear-capable bomber force, including the B-52 Stratofortress and B-2 Spirit, Feb. 1, 2010 (top photo). U.S. Air Force photo. An unarmed Minuteman III intercontinental ballistic missile is test launched off the California coast (bottom right photo). U.S. Air Force photo. The U.S. Navy's nuclear ballistic missile submarine USS MAINE (SSBN-741) conducts surface navigational operations (bottom left photo). Photo by PH1 Michael J. Rinaldi.

Each leg of the Triad has advantages that warrant retaining all three legs at this stage of reductions. Strategic nuclear submarines (SSBNs) and the SLBMs they carry represent the most survivable leg of the U.S. nuclear Triad. Today, there appears to be no viable near or mid-term threats to the survivability of U.S. SSBNs, but such threats – or other technical problems – cannot be ruled out over the long term. Single-warhead ICBMs contribute to stability, and like SLBMs are not vulnerable to air defenses. Unlike ICBMs and SLBMs, bombers can be visibly deployed forward, as a signal in crisis to strengthen deterrence of potential adversaries and assurance of allies and partners.

While significantly reducing the size of the technical hedge overall, the United States will retain the ability to "upload" some nuclear warheads as a technical hedge against any future problems with U.S. delivery systems or warheads, or as a result of a fundamental deterioration of the security environment. For example, if there were a problem with a specific ICBM warhead type, it could be taken out of service and replaced with warheads from another ICBM warhead type, and/or nuclear warheads could be uploaded on SLBMs and/or bombers.

Sustaining Strategic Submarines (SSBNs)

The NPR concluded that ensuring a survivable U.S. response force requires continuous at-sea deployments of SSBNs in both the Atlantic and Pacific oceans, as well as the ability to surge additional submarines in crisis. To support this requirement, the United States currently has fourteen nuclear-capable Ohio-class SSBNs.

By 2020, Ohio-class submarines will have been in service longer than any previous submarines. Therefore as a prudent hedge, the Navy will retain all 14 SSBNs for the near-term. Depending on future force structure assessments, and on how remaining SSBNs age in the coming years, the United States will consider reducing from 14 to 12 Ohio-class submarines in the second half of this decade. This decision will not affect the number of deployed nuclear warheads on SSBNs.

To maintain an at-sea presence for the long-term, the United States must continue development of a follow-on to the Ohio-class submarine. The first Ohio-class submarine retirement is planned for 2027. Since the lead times associated with designing, building, testing, and deploying new submarines are particularly long, the Secretary of Defense has directed the Navy to begin technology development of an SSBN replacement.

Chief Torpedoman Eric Ragan looks through binoculars while watching for a personnel transfer vessel to welcome the newest members of the crew aboard nuclear ballistic missile submarine USS Louisiana (SSBN 743). U.S. Navy photo by Electronics Technician 3rd Class Dominique Cardenas.

Today, there appears to be no credible near or mid-term threats to the survivability of U.S. SSBNs. However, given the stakes involved, the Department of Defense will continue a robust SSBN Security Program that aims to anticipate potential threats and develop appropriate countermeasures to protect current and future SSBNs.

A "DeMIRVed" ICBM Force

Today, the United States has 450 deployed silo-based Minuteman III ICBMs, each with one to three warheads. The NPR considered the type and number of ICBMs needed for stable deterrence, and to serve as a hedge against any future vulnerability of U.S. SSBNs.

The United States will "deMIRV" all deployed ICBMs, so that each Minuteman III ICBM has only one nuclear warhead. (A "MIRVed" ballistic missile carries Multiple Independently-targetable Reentry Vehicles (MIRVs). "DeMIRVing" will reduce each missile to a single warhead.) This step will enhance the stability of the nuclear balance by reducing the incentives for either side to strike first.

ICBMs provide significant advantages to the U.S. nuclear force posture, including extremely secure command and control, high readiness rates, and relatively low operating costs. The Department of Defense will continue the Minuteman III Life Extension Program with the aim of keeping the fleet in service to 2030, as mandated by Congress. Although a decision on any follow-on ICBM is not needed for several years, studies to inform that decision are needed now. Accordingly, the Department of Defense will begin initial study of alternatives in fiscal years (FY) 2011 and 2012. This study will consider a range of possible deployment options, with the objective of defining a cost-effective approach that supports continued reductions in U.S. nuclear weapons while promoting stable deterrence.

A Smaller and Highly Capable Nuclear Bomber Force

U.S. Air Force Capt. Joshua Logie, a B-52 Stratofortress pilot assigned to the 20th Expeditionary Bomb Squadron, Barksdale Air Force Base, completes a flight on Feb. 9, 2010. U.S. Air Force photo by Staff Sgt. Jacob N. Bailey.

The United States currently has 76 B-52H bombers and 18 B-2 bombers that can be equipped with nuclear weapons. The NPR determined that the Air Force will retain nuclear-capable bombers, while converting some B-52Hs to a conventional-only role.

There are two principal reasons to retain nuclear-capable – or more accurately dual-capable – bombers. First, this capability provides a rapid and effective hedge against technical challenges with another leg of the Triad, as well as geopolitical uncertainties. Second, nuclear-capable bombers are important to extended deterrence of potential attacks on U.S. allies and partners. Unlike ICBMs and SLBMs, heavy bombers can be visibly forward deployed, thereby signaling U.S. resolve and commitment in crisis.

U.S. dual-capable heavy bombers will not be placed on full-time nuclear alert, and so will provide additional conventional firepower. The value of heavy bombers has been demonstrated multiple times since World War II, including in Desert Storm, Kosovo, Operation Iraqi Freedom, and Operation Enduring Freedom. The Department of Defense (DoD) will invest more than $1 billion over the next five years to support upgrades to the B-2 stealth bomber. These enhancements will help sustain survivability and improve mission effectiveness.

DoD is studying the appropriate mix of long-range strike capabilities, including heavy bombers as well as non-nuclear prompt global strike, in follow-on analysis to the 2010 Quadrennial Defense Review and the NPR. This analysis will affect the Department's FY 2012 budget proposal. In addition, the Air Force will conduct an assessment of alternatives to inform decisions in FY 2012 about whether and (if so) how to replace the current air-launched cruise missile (ALCM), which will reach the end of its service life later in the next decade.

DoD is also studying emerging challenges in the defense industrial base. As commitments are made to life extend or replace current weapons, challenges are likely to emerge that could impair needed progress. Steps can be taken now to mitigate some of these risks. An example is in the production of solid rocket motors. Across the U.S. Government, there are three users of the solid rocket motor industry: the National Aeronautics and Space Administration (NASA) for shuttle boosters; the Air Force for Minuteman III, and the Navy for Trident II D-5. None of them has immediate plans for a new large solid rocket motor design. With current plans to sustain the

Minuteman III and Trident II strategic missiles for at least another two decades, the nation will need technically skilled personnel to address the unknown future challenges associated with the aging of these systems. In order to revive the health of this industry, a research and development program is being initiated that focuses on commonality between the Military Departments and joint scalable flight test demonstrations.

In sum, the NPR concluded:

- Stable deterrence can be maintained while reducing accountable U.S. strategic delivery vehicles by approximately 50 percent from the START level and reducing accountable strategic warheads by approximately 30 percent from the 2002 Moscow Treaty level.

- During the ten-year duration of New START, the nuclear Triad of ICBMs, SLBMs, and heavy bombers will be maintained.

- All U.S. ICBMs will be "de-MIRVed" to a single warhead each to increase stability.

- Some ability to "upload" non-deployed nuclear weapons on existing delivery vehicles should be retained as a hedge against technical or geopolitical surprise. Preference will be given to upload capacity for bombers and strategic submarines.

- Contributions by non-nuclear systems to U.S. regional deterrence and reassurance goals will be preserved by avoiding limitations on missile defenses in New START and ensuring that New START will not preclude options for using heavy bombers or long-range missile systems in conventional roles.

The NPR conducted extensive analysis of alternative force structures under a New START Treaty, and the Department of Defense will define its planned force structure under the Treaty after taking account of this work. The United States will retain the ability to adjust this posture under New START as needed to account for unexpected technological developments or operational vulnerabilities, or geo-political surprise.

Maximizing Presidential Decision Time

Maximizing decision time for the President can further strengthen strategic stability at lower force levels. Thus, the NPR considered changes to existing nuclear policies and postures that directly affect potential crisis stability, including alert postures and the Nuclear Command, Control, and Communication (NC3) system.

The NPR examined possible adjustments to the current alert posture of U.S. strategic forces. Today, U.S. nuclear-capable heavy bombers are off full-time alert, nearly all ICBMs remain on alert, and a significant number of SSBNs are at sea at any given time. The NPR concluded that this posture should be maintained.

The NPR reaffirmed the current practice of "open-ocean targeting" of all ICBMs and SLBMs so that, in the highly unlikely event of an accidental launch, the missile would land in the open ocean. The United States will ask Russia to reaffirm its commitment to continue this practice, which was mutually agreed in 1994.

Capt. Jeremy Ritter, 490th Missile Squadron (MS) flight commander (right), and 1st Lt. William Springer, 490th MS ICBM combat crew deputy commander (left), are "strapped in" and coordinating with the other launch crews to turn keys to launch their missiles during a simulation in the Missile Procedure Trainer. Crews "strap in" to prevent being thrown around the capsule in the event that they are attacked. U.S. Air Force photo by John Turner.

The NPR considered the possibility of reducing alert rates for ICBMs and at-sea rates of SSBNs, and concluded that such steps could reduce crisis stability by giving an adversary the incentive to attack before "re-alerting" was complete. At the same time, the NPR concluded that returning heavy bombers to full-time nuclear alert was not necessary, assuming the other two Triad legs retained a significant alert rate.

Looking to the longer term, the NPR initiated studies that may lead to future reductions in alert posture. For example, in an initial study of possible follow-on systems to the Minuteman III ICBM force, the Department of Defense will explore whether new modes of basing may ensure the survivability of this leg of the Triad while eliminating or reducing incentives for prompt launch.

Additionally, the NPR examined the effectiveness of our command and control of U.S. nuclear forces as an essential element in ensuring crisis stability, deterrence, and the safety, security and effectiveness of our nuclear stockpile. The DoD NC3 system enables informed and timely decisions by the President, the sole authority for nuclear employment, and execution of Presidential nuclear response options.

The Secretary of Defense has directed a number of initiatives to further improve the resiliency of the NC3 system and the capabilities for the fully deliberative control of the force in time of crisis. The Department of Defense has taken steps to strengthen NC3 in the FY 2011 budget request, including modernizing "legacy" single-purpose NC3 capabilities to meet current and projected challenges, and continuing to invest in secure voice conferences for NC3. An interagency study is being initiated to determine the investment needed and the organizational structure best suited to further strengthen the NC3 capabilities. This study, led by DoD, will begin in 2010 and provide a long-term strategy that will inform out-year budget submission to Congress.

The NPR concluded that the United States will:

- Maintain the current alert posture of U.S. strategic forces: U.S. nuclear-capable heavy bombers off full-time alert, nearly all ICBMs on alert, and a significant number of SSBNs at sea at any given time.

- Continue the practice of "open-ocean targeting" of all ICBMs and SLBMs so that, in the highly unlikely event of an unauthorized or accidental launch, the missile would land in the open ocean. The United States will ask Russia to re-confirm its commitment to this practice.

- Make new investments in the U.S. command and control system to maximize Presidential decision time in a nuclear crisis.

- Explore new modes of ICBM basing that could enhance survivability and further reduce any incentives for prompt launch. Such an assessment will be part of the Department of Defense's study of possible replacements for the current ICBM force.

Non-Strategic Nuclear Weapons

The United States has reduced its non-strategic (or "tactical") nuclear weapons dramatically since the end of the Cold War. Today, it keeps only a limited number of forward deployed nuclear weapons in Europe, plus a small number of nuclear weapons stored in the United States, available for global deployment in support of extended deterrence to allies and partners. Russia maintains a much larger force of non-strategic nuclear weapons, a significant number of which are deployed near the territories of several North Atlantic Treaty Organization (NATO) countries and are therefore a concern to NATO.

Non-strategic nuclear weapons, together with the non-deployed nuclear weapons of both sides, should be included in any future reduction arrangements between the United States and Russia. The United States will consult with our allies regarding the future basing of nuclear weapons in Europe, and is committed to making consensus decisions through NATO processes. In cooperation with allies and partners, the NPR has determined that the following steps will be taken.

- The Air Force will retain a dual-capable fighter (the capability to deliver both conventional and nuclear weapons) as it replaces F-16s with the F-35 Joint Strike Fighter. As described in more detail below, the United States will also conduct a full scope B-61 (nuclear bomb) Life Extension Program to ensure its functionality with the F-35 and to include making surety – safety, security, and use control – enhancements to maintain confidence in the B-61. These decisions ensure that the United States will retain the capability to forward-deploy non-strategic nuclear weapons in support of its Alliance commitments. These decisions do not presume the results of future decisions within

NATO about the requirements of nuclear deterrence and nuclear sharing, but keep open all options.

- The United States will retire the nuclear-equipped sea-launched cruise missile (TLAM-N). This system serves a redundant purpose in the U.S. nuclear stockpile. It has been one of a number of means to forward-deploy nuclear weapons in time of crisis. Other means include forward-deployment of bombers with either bombs or cruise missiles, as well as forward-deployment of dual-capable fighters. In addition, U.S. ICBMs and SLBMs are capable of striking any potential adversary. The deterrence and assurance roles of TLAM-N can be adequately substituted by these other means, and the United States remains committed to providing a credible extended deterrence posture and capabilities.

As these NPR decisions are implemented and as we work with our allies and partners to strengthen security while reducing the role and numbers of nuclear weapons, we will continue close consultations with allies and partners. No changes to U.S. extended deterrence capabilities will be made without continued close consultation with allies and partners.

These decisions are embedded in a broader approach to the emerging challenges of extended deterrence that is reflected in not just the NPR but also the 2010 Ballistic Missile Defense Review (BMDR) and 2010 Quadrennial Defense Review (QDR). The United States seeks to significantly strengthen regional security architectures in a comprehensive way. It seeks improved peacetime approaches that fully integrate "whole of government" approaches as well as the "hard" and "soft power" tools of the United States and its allies and partners, including an overall balance of conventional military power that serves the purposes of security and peace. U.S. nuclear weapons will play a role in the deterrence of regional states so long as those states have nuclear weapons, but the decisions taken in the NPR, BMDR, and QDR reflect the U.S. desire to increase reliance on non-nuclear means to accomplish our objectives of deterring such states and reassuring our allies and partners.

Reinforcing Strategic Stability

Given that Russia and China are currently modernizing their nuclear capabilities – and that both are claiming U.S. missile defense and conventionally-armed missile programs are destabilizing – maintaining strategic stability with the two countries will be an important challenge in the years ahead.

- The United States will therefore pursue high-level, bilateral dialogues with Russia and China aimed at promoting more stable, resilient, and transparent strategic relationships.

A strategic dialogue with Russia will allow the United States to explain that our missile defenses and any future U.S. conventionally-armed long-range ballistic missile systems are designed to address newly emerging regional threats, and are not intended to affect the strategic balance with

Russia. For its part, Russia could explain its modernization programs, clarify its current military doctrine (especially the extent to which it places importance on nuclear weapons), and discuss steps it could take to allay concerns in the West about its non-strategic nuclear arsenal, such as further consolidating its non-strategic systems in a small number of secure facilities deep within Russia.

A bilateral dialogue would also provide an opportunity for the two sides to consider wide-ranging missile defense cooperation, building on a joint statement signed by President Obama and President Medvedev in July 2009, and addressing such areas as integrating U.S. and Russian sensors, developing joint missile defense architectures, and conducting joint testing, research and development, modeling and simulations, and exercises.

U.S. Navy Adm. Mike Mullen, Chairman of the Joint Chiefs of Staff, and Gen. Nikolai Makarov, Chief of the Russian Armed Forces General Staff, address the media after counterpart talks in Moscow, Russia June 26, 2009. DoD photo by Mass Communication Specialist 1st Class Chad J. McNeeley.

With China, the purpose of a dialogue on strategic stability is to provide a venue and mechanism for each side to communicate its views about the other's strategies, policies, and programs on nuclear weapons and other strategic capabilities. The goal of such a dialogue is to enhance confidence, improve transparency, and reduce mistrust. As stated in the 2010 Ballistic Missile Defense Review Report, "maintaining strategic stability in the U.S.-China relationship is as important to this Administration as maintaining strategic stability with other major powers."

Building more stable strategic relationships with Russia and China could contribute to greater restraint in those countries' nuclear programs and postures, which could have a reassuring and stabilizing effect in their regions. It could also facilitate closer cooperation by those two countries with the United States on measures to prevent nuclear proliferation and nuclear terrorism.

Future Nuclear Reductions

The United States is committed to the long-term goal of a world free of nuclear weapons. The President has directed a review of potential future reductions in U.S. nuclear weapons below New START levels. Several factors will influence the magnitude and pace of such reductions.

First, any future nuclear reductions must continue to strengthen deterrence of potential regional adversaries, strategic stability vis-à-vis Russia and China, and assurance of our allies and partners.

This will require an updated assessment of deterrence requirements; further improvements in U.S., allied, and partner non-nuclear capabilities; focused reductions in strategic and non-strategic weapons; and close consultations with allies and partners. The United States will continue to ensure that, in the calculations of any potential opponent, the perceived gains of attacking the United States or its allies and partners would be far outweighed by the unacceptable costs of the response.

Second, implementation of the Stockpile Stewardship Program and the nuclear infrastructure investments recommended in the NPR will allow the United States to shift away from retaining large numbers of non-deployed warheads as a hedge against technical or geopolitical surprise, allowing major reductions in the nuclear stockpile. These investments are essential to facilitating reductions while sustaining deterrence under New START and beyond.

Third, Russia's nuclear force will remain a significant factor in determining how much and how fast we are prepared to reduce U.S. forces. Following ratification and entry into force of New START, the Administration will pursue a follow-on agreement with Russia that binds both countries to further reductions in all nuclear weapons. Because of our improved relations, the need for strict numerical parity between the two countries is no longer as compelling as it was during the Cold War. But large disparities in nuclear capabilities could raise concerns on both sides and among U.S. allies and partners, and may not be conducive to maintaining a stable, long-term strategic relationship, especially as nuclear forces are significantly reduced. Therefore, we will place importance on Russia joining us as we move to lower levels.

The President has directed follow-on analysis to the NPR that considers the above three factors, and others as appropriate, to set goals for future U.S.-Russia reductions in nuclear weapons below New START levels. The size and pace of U.S. nuclear force reductions will be implemented in ways that maintain the reliability and effectiveness of our security assurances to our allies and partners.

Following ratification and entry into force of New START, the Administration will pursue discussions with Russia on further reductions and transparency, which could be pursued through formal agreements and/or parallel voluntary measures. These follow-on reductions should be broader in scope than previous bilateral agreements, addressing all the nuclear weapons of the two countries, not just deployed strategic nuclear weapons.

STRENGTHENING REGIONAL DETERRENCE AND REASSURING U.S. ALLIES AND PARTNERS

U.S. allies and partners are on the front lines of a changing global security environment. Some are enjoying unprecedented security and accordingly seek an acceleration of efforts to reduce reliance on nuclear deterrence. Others face new challenges to their security and look to the United States for continued partnership in safeguarding their interests. Among their neighbors are nuclear proliferators, potential smugglers of weapons of mass destruction (WMD), and weak and failing states. Some also feel the pressures of neighboring major powers asserting stronger regional roles, in some cases by nuclear means.

An F-35 Joint Strike Fighter test aircraft undergoes a flight check over Fort Worth, Texas. U.S. Air Force photo courtesy of Lockheed Martin.

Accordingly, the United States is fully committed to strengthening bilateral and regional security ties and working closely with its allies and partners to adapt these relationships to emerging 21st century requirements. We will continue to assure our allies and partners of our commitment to their security and to demonstrate this commitment not only through words, but also through deeds. This includes the continued forward deployment of U.S. forces in key regions, strengthening of U.S. and allied non-nuclear capabilities, and the continued provision of extended deterrence. Such security relationships are critical not only in deterring potential threats, but can also serve our non-proliferation goals – by demonstrating to neighboring states that their pursuit of nuclear weapons will only undermine their goal of achieving military or political advantages, and by reassuring non-nuclear U.S. allies and partners that their security interests can be protected without their own nuclear deterrent capabilities. Further, the United States will work with allies and partners to strengthen the global non-proliferation regime, especially the implementation of existing commitments within their regions.

Security architectures in key regions will retain a nuclear dimension as long as nuclear threats to U.S. allies and partners remain. U.S. nuclear weapons have played an essential role in extending deterrence to U.S. allies and partners against nuclear attacks or nuclear-backed coercion by states in their region that possess or are seeking nuclear weapons. A credible U.S. "nuclear umbrella" has been provided by a combination of means – the strategic forces of the U.S. Triad, non-strategic nuclear weapons deployed forward in key regions, and U.S.-based nuclear weapons that could be deployed forward quickly to meet regional contingencies.

The mix of deterrence means has varied over time and from region to region. During the Cold War, the United States forward-deployed nuclear weapons in both Europe and Asia, and retained the capability to increase those deployments if needed. At the end of the Cold War, a series of steps were taken to dramatically reduce the forward presence of U.S. nuclear weapons. Today, there are separate choices to be made in partnership with allies in Europe and Asia about what posture best serves our shared interests in deterrence and assurance and in moving toward a world of reduced nuclear dangers.

In Europe, forward-deployed U.S. nuclear weapons have been reduced dramatically since the end of the Cold War, but a small number of U.S. nuclear weapons remain. Although the risk of nuclear attack against North Atlantic Treaty Organization (NATO) members is at an historic low, the presence of U.S. nuclear weapons – combined with NATO's unique nuclear sharing arrangements under which non-nuclear members participate in nuclear planning and possess specially configured aircraft capable of delivering nuclear weapons – contribute to Alliance cohesion and provide reassurance to allies and partners who feel exposed to regional threats. The role of nuclear weapons in defending Alliance members will be discussed this year in connection with NATO's revision of its Strategic Concept. Any changes in NATO's nuclear posture should only be taken after a thorough review within – and decision by – the Alliance.

In Asia and the Middle East – where there are no multilateral alliance structures analogous to NATO – the United States has mainly extended deterrence through bilateral alliances and security relationships and through its forward military presence and security guarantees. When the Cold War ended, the United States withdrew its forward-deployed nuclear weapons from the Pacific region, including removing nuclear weapons from naval surface vessels and general purpose submarines. Since then, it has relied on its central strategic forces and the capacity to re-deploy non-strategic nuclear systems in East Asia, if needed, in times of crisis.

The Administration is pursuing strategic dialogues with its allies and partners in East Asia and the Middle East to determine how best to cooperatively strengthen regional security architectures to enhance peace and security, and reassure them that U.S. extended deterrence is credible and effective.

Regional Security Architectures

Enhancing regional security architectures is a key part of the U.S. strategy for strengthening regional deterrence while reducing the role and numbers of nuclear weapons. These regional security architectures include effective missile defense, counter-WMD capabilities, conventional power-projection capabilities, and integrated command and control – all underwritten by strong political commitments. The goal is to ensure that if states attempt to attack U.S. forces or our allies and partners, their attacks will be blunted and their aims denied by an enhanced set of capabilities – and that these states understand this reality and so are deterred from threatening or undertaking such an attack.

Strengthening the non-nuclear elements of regional security architectures is vital to moving toward a world free of nuclear weapons. The United States is positioned with capabilities across all domains to deter a wide range of attacks or forms of coercion against itself, its allies, and partners. Credible deterrence depends on land, air, and naval forces capable of fighting limited and large-scale conflicts in anti-access environments, as well as forces prepared to respond to the full range of challenges posed by state and non-state groups. These forces are enabled by U.S. capabilities to protect its assets in cyberspace and outer space and enhanced by U.S. capabilities to deny adversaries' objectives through resilient infrastructure (including command and control systems), global basing and posture, and ballistic missile defense and counter-WMD capabilities.

Effective missile defenses are an essential element of the U.S. commitment to strengthen regional deterrence against states of concern. Thus, while the United States will maintain a nuclear deterrent to cope with such states, we are also bolstering the other critical elements of U.S. deterrence, including conventional and ballistic missile defense capabilities.

The U.S. nuclear posture has a vital role to play in regional security architectures. Proliferating states must understand that any attack on the United States, or our allies and partners, will be defeated, and any use of nuclear weapons will be met with a response that would be effective and overwhelming. The President, as Commander-in-Chief, will determine the precise nature of any U.S. response. But by pursuing nuclear weapons, such states must understand that they have significantly raised the stakes of any conflict.

Key Initiatives

Enduring alliances and broad-based political relationships are the foundation of strategic stability and security. The United States will work closely with allies and partners across the globe to ensure strong political and military ties, based on a common understanding of the challenges and opportunities of the emerging security environment, and strengthen regional deterrence. The United States will:

- Continue to work extensively with allies and partners to build enhanced regional security architectures, including non-nuclear capabilities for deterrence, helping to build partner capacity, conducting combined exercises and training, and sustaining a forward presence in key regions – as described in the 2010 Quadrennial Defense Review (QDR) and the 2010 Ballistic Missile Defense Review (BMDR).

- Continue and, where appropriate, expand ongoing bilateral and multilateral discussions with allies and partners, including in Europe, Northeast Asia, Southwest Asia, and the Middle East, on the most effective ways to enhance regional stability in the near-term and long-term.

- Work with allies and partners to respond to regional threats by deploying effective missile defenses, including in Europe, Northeast Asia, the Middle East, and Southwest Asia. This includes pursuing a Phased Adaptive Approach in these regions – as described in detail in the 2010 BMDR.

- Strengthen counter-WMD capabilities, including improved U.S. and allied ability to defeat chemical or biological attack. The Department of Defense is significantly bolstering defenses against next-generation chemical weapons and advanced biological weapons – these initiatives are described in more detail in the 2010 QDR.

Members of a joint U.S. and Australian Navy boarding team conduct a security sweep aboard USNS Walter S. Diehl (T-AO 193), Oct. 29, 2009, during a boarding exercise in the South China Sea as part of the Proliferation Security Initiative (PSI) exercise Deep Sabre II. DoD photo by Mass Communication Spc. 2nd Class Seth Clarke.

- Develop non-nuclear prompt global strike capabilities. These capabilities may be particularly valuable for the defeat of time-urgent regional threats. The Administration is currently examining the appropriate mix of such capabilities needed to improve our ability to address such regional threats, while not negatively affecting the stability of our nuclear relationships with Russia or China. Specific recommendations will be made in the fiscal year (FY) 2012 Department of Defense budget.

- Develop and deploy, over the next decade, more effective capabilities for real-time intelligence, surveillance, and reconnaissance capabilities, as well as intelligence analysis to enable rapid processing of data.

- Expand and deepen consultations with allies and partners on policies and combined postures to prevent proliferation and credibly deter aggression.

- Retain the capability to forward-deploy U.S. nuclear weapons on tactical fighter-bombers (in the future, the F-35 Joint Strike Fighter) and heavy bombers (the B-2 and B-52H), and will proceed with full scope life extension, including surety – safety, security, and use control – enhancements, for the B-61 nuclear bomb, which will be able to be carried by the F-35 and B-2. These decisions do not presume what NATO will decide about future deterrence requirements, but are intended to keep the Alliance's options open and provide capabilities to support other U.S. commitments.

SUSTAINING A SAFE, SECURE, AND EFFECTIVE NUCLEAR ARSENAL

The United States is committed to ensuring that the nuclear weapons stockpile remains safe, secure, and effective. The NPR has made a significant number of decisions to meet this long-term obligation.

Today's nuclear weapons have aged well beyond their originally planned lifetime. Until 1992, the U.S. nuclear stockpile was sustained through continual warhead-type replacement that proceeded from design to test, deployment, and then retirement and replacement by a successor design. Since then, the United States has stopped testing nuclear weapons, maintaining and certifying our warheads as safe and reliable through a Stockpile Stewardship Program that has extended the lives of some warheads by refurbishing them to nearly original specifications.

To sustain a safe, secure, and effective stockpile today, with the ultimate goal of a world free of nuclear weapons in the future, we must prudently manage our nuclear stockpile and related Life Extension Programs (LEPs), while cultivating the nuclear infrastructure, expert workforce, and leadership required to sustain it.

Managing the U.S. Nuclear Stockpile

The U.S. nuclear stockpile includes both deployed and non-deployed warheads. The United States has additional warheads awaiting dismantlement.

Deployed warheads include both strategic (planned to be delivered at intercontinental range and deployed on strategic submarines (SSBNs), intercontinental ballistic missiles (ICBMs), and heavy bombers) and non-strategic weapons assigned a nuclear mission, such as the B-61 bombs deployed in Europe. In the near- to mid-term, the U.S. strategic deployed force

Secretary of Energy Steven Chu speaks at a dedication ceremony recognizing the start-up of operations at the nation's new facility for weapons-grade uranium. The Highly Enriched Uranium Materials Facility (HEUMF) – the ultra-secure uranium warehouse at the Y-12 National Security Complex – replaces multiple aging buildings with a single state-of-the-art storage facility. NNSA photo.

will be reduced through arms control agreements with Russia, initially by the New Strategic Arms Reduction Treaty (New START).

Non-deployed warheads provide logistics spares, support the surveillance program, and hedge against technical or geopolitical surprise. Logistics spares enable the United States to maintain desired quantities of deployed weapons during maintenance and surveillance where some warhead components are destroyed and the warheads are not rebuilt for return to the stockpile. Non-deployed warheads also provide a hedge against technological surprise, such as discovery of a technical problem in a warhead that renders it (and all of its type) non-operational. They also serve as a hedge against geopolitical surprise, such as an erosion of the security environment that requires additional weapons to be uploaded on delivery systems. The non-deployed stockpile currently includes more warheads than required for the above purposes, due to the limited capacity of the National Nuclear Security Administration (NNSA) complex to conduct LEPs for deployed weapons in a timely manner. Progress in restoring NNSA's production infrastructure will allow these excess warheads to be retired along with other stockpile reductions planned over the next decade.

Warheads awaiting dismantlement are those in the queue for disassembly. Today, there are several thousand nuclear warheads awaiting dismantlement, and this number will increase as weapons are removed from the stockpile under New START. We anticipate it will take more than a decade to eliminate the dismantlement backlog. Investments to modernize the nuclear infrastructure, outlined below, will ensure that the United States can continue to decrease this backlog in a responsible manner.

Looking ahead three decades, the NPR considered how best to extend the lives of existing nuclear warheads consistent with the congressionally mandated Stockpile Management Program and U.S. non-proliferation goals. Over that period, every nuclear warhead now in the stockpile will require some level of technical attention. Thus, the Stockpile Management Program will outline ways to ensure the safety and security of warheads over time. While the general parameters of this plan are discussed here, some key information about the specific numbers and types of warheads in different elements of the stockpile are classified, as are specific plans for their future disposition, and will be briefed separately to Congress.

After consideration of how to best manage our current stockpile, the NPR reached the following conclusions to guide future U.S. stockpile management decisions:

- The United States will not conduct nuclear testing, and will pursue ratification and entry into force of the Comprehensive Nuclear Test Ban Treaty.

- The United States will not develop new nuclear warheads. Life Extension Programs will use only nuclear components based on previously tested designs, and will not support new military missions or provide for new military capabilities.

- The United States will study options for ensuring the safety, security, and reliability of nuclear warheads on a case-by-case basis, consistent with the congressionally mandated Stockpile Management Program. The full range of LEP approaches will be considered: refurbishment of existing warheads, reuse of nuclear components from different warheads, and replacement of nuclear components.

- In any decision to proceed to engineering development for warhead LEPs, the United States will give strong preference to options for refurbishment or reuse. Replacement of nuclear components would be undertaken only if critical Stockpile Management Program goals could not otherwise be met, and if specifically authorized by the President and approved by Congress.

- The United States will retain the smallest possible nuclear stockpile consistent with our need to deter adversaries, reassure our allies, and hedge against technical or geopolitical surprise.

Using these guidelines, the United States will extend the life of nuclear warheads required for the smaller force structure identified under New START. Consistent with this approach, the NPR recommended that:

- The Administration will fully fund the ongoing LEP for the W-76 submarine-based warhead for a fiscal year (FY) 2017 completion, and the full scope LEP study and follow-on activities for the B-61 bomb to ensure first production begins in FY 2017.

- The Nuclear Weapons Council will initiate a study in 2010 of LEP options for the W-78 ICBM warhead to be conducted jointly by the National Nuclear Security Administration and the Department of Defense. This study will consider, as all future LEP studies will, the possibility of using the resulting warhead also on multiple platforms in order to reduce the number of warhead types.

Air Force maintenance technicians work on the B-61 bomb. U.S. Air Force photo.

- The United States will consider reductions in non-deployed nuclear warheads, as well as acceleration of the pace of nuclear warhead dismantlement, as it implements a new stockpile stewardship and management plan consistent with New START.

The National Nuclear Security Administration (NNSA), in close coordination with DoD, will provide a new stockpile stewardship and management plan to Congress within 90 days, consistent with the increases in infrastructure investment requested in the President's FY 2011 budget. As critical infrastructure is restored and modernized, it will allow the United States to begin to shift away from retaining large numbers of non-deployed warheads as a technical hedge, allowing additional reductions in the U.S. stockpile of non-deployed nuclear weapons over time.

The approach described here will ensure high confidence in the technical performance of warheads retained in the stockpile. It will guarantee that their safety and security are aligned with 21st century requirements (and technical capabilities). At the same time, it will not develop new nuclear warheads, and it will be structured so as not to require nuclear testing. Life Extension Programs will use only nuclear components based on previously tested designs, and will not support new military missions or provide for new military capabilities. This approach sets a high standard for the safety and security of U.S. nuclear weapons and, in support of nonproliferation goals, positions the United States to encourage other nations to maintain the highest levels of surety for their nuclear stockpiles.

Critical Infrastructure and Human Capital

In order to sustain a safe, secure, and effective U.S. nuclear stockpile as long as nuclear weapons exist, the United States must possess a modern physical infrastructure – comprised of the national security laboratories and a complex of supporting facilities – and a highly capable workforce with the specialized skills needed to sustain the nuclear deterrent and support the President's nuclear security agenda.

Today's nuclear complex, however, has fallen into neglect. Although substantial science, technology, and engineering investments were made over the last decade under the auspices of the Stockpile Stewardship Program, the complex still includes many oversized and costly-to-maintain facilities built during the 1940s and 1950s. Some facilities needed for working with plutonium and uranium date back to the Manhattan Project. Safety, security, and environmental issues associated with these aging facilities are mounting, as are the costs of addressing them.

Responsible stockpile management and disarmament require not only infrastructure, but skilled scientists and engineers to manage these efforts. Like our infrastructure, over the last decade our human capital base has been underfunded and underdeveloped. Our national security laboratories have found it increasingly difficult to attract and retain the best and brightest scientists and engineers of today. Morale has declined with the lack of broad, national consensus on the approach to sustaining warheads and nuclear technical capabilities. The cumulative loss of focus, expertise, and excellence on nuclear matters in the United States remains a significant challenge. A strong national commitment to these important nuclear security objectives is essential to countering this trend.

Increased investments in the nuclear infrastructure and a highly skilled workforce are needed to ensure the long-term safety, security, and effectiveness of our nuclear arsenal and to support the full range of nuclear security work to include non-proliferation, nuclear forensics, nuclear, counter-terrorism, emergency management, intelligence analysis and treaty verification.

Such investments, over time, can reduce our reliance on large inventories of non-deployed warheads to deal with technical surprise, thereby allowing additional reductions in the U.S. nuclear stockpile and supporting our long-term path to zero. A revitalized infrastructure will also serve to reduce the number of warheads retained as a geopolitical hedge, by helping to dissuade potential competitors from believing they can permanently secure an advantage by deploying new nuclear capabilities.

Efforts to strengthen the science, technology, and engineering base and address the problems in the physical infrastructure will help with the human capital problem. A renewal of the sense of national purpose and direction in nuclear strategy will also be helpful. The President has clearly outlined the importance of nuclear issues for our national security, and the importance of keeping the U.S. nuclear deterrent safe, secure, and effective at the minimum numbers required. Further, the Administration's commitment to a clear and long-term plan for managing the stockpile ensures the scientists and engineers of tomorrow will have the opportunity to engage in challenging research and development activities which is essential to their recruitment and retention.

A modern nuclear infrastructure and highly skilled workforce is not only consistent with our arms control and non-proliferation objectives; it is essential to them. By certifying the reliability of each weapon type we retain, the United States can credibly assure non-nuclear allies and partners they need not build their own, while

Aerial photo of the Y-12 National Security Complex, in Oak Ridge, Tennessee. Y-12 plays a vital role in the Department of Energy's Nuclear Security Enterprise helping ensure a safe and reliable U.S. nuclear weapons deterrent. Y-12 also retrieves and stores nuclear materials, fuels the nation's naval reactors and performs complementary work for other government and private-sector entities. Y-12 photo.

seeking greater stockpile reductions than otherwise possible. Further, a corps of highly skilled personnel will continue to expand our ability to understand the technical challenges associated with verifying ever deeper arms control reductions.

Through science and engineering programs that improve the analysis of the reliability of our warheads, we also enhance our ability to assess and render safe potential terrorist nuclear devices and support other national security initiatives, such as nuclear forensics and attribution. Expert nuclear scientists and engineers help improve our understanding of foreign nuclear weapons activities, which is critical for managing risks on the path to zero. And, in a world with complete nuclear disarmament, a robust intellectual and physical capability would provide the ultimate insurance against nuclear break-out by an aggressor.

Additionally, the industrial base activities that support the nuclear enterprise also remain critical to the nation's deterrence posture. Increased surveillance of critical commercial sector human skills, manufacturing capabilities, and sustainment capabilities is required to ensure this infrastructure remains viable to support the enterprise.

The NPR concluded that the following key investments were required to sustain a safe, secure, and effective nuclear arsenal:

- Strengthening the science, technology, and engineering (ST&E) base needed for conducting weapon system LEPs, maturing advanced technologies to increase weapons surety, qualification of weapon components and certifying weapons without nuclear testing, and providing annual stockpile assessments through weapons surveillance. This includes developing and sustaining high quality scientific staff and supporting computational and experimental capabilities. The NNSA will develop a long-term strategy that will describe the ST&E base required to meet the Stockpile Stewardship Program. The report will be delivered to the Nuclear Weapons Council in 2011.

- Funding the Chemistry and Metallurgy Research Replacement Project at Los Alamos National Laboratory to replace the existing 50-year old Chemistry and Metallurgy Research facility in 2021.

- Developing a new Uranium Processing Facility at the Y-12 Plant in Oak Ridge, Tennessee to come on line for production operations in 2021. Without an ability to produce uranium components, any plan to sustain the stockpile, as well as support for our Navy nuclear propulsion, will come to a halt. This would have a significant impact, not just on the weapons program, but in dealing with nuclear dangers of many kinds.

More broadly, the Administration supports the needed recapitalization of the nuclear infrastructure through fully funding the NNSA. New production facilities will be sized to support the requirements of the Stockpile Stewardship Program mandated by Congress and to meet the multiple requirements of dismantling warheads and eliminating material no longer needed for defense purposes, conducting technical surveillance, implementing life extension plans, and supporting naval requirements. Some modest capacity will be put in place to surge production in the event of significant geopolitical "surprise."

Defense Department Leadership of the Nuclear Deterrence Mission

Sustaining a safe, secure, and effective nuclear arsenal requires sustained and effective leadership. In recent years, it has been necessary for the Department of Defense to renew its commitment to that leadership, following the cumulative loss of focus and expertise on nuclear matters within DoD. The Department has taken a number of steps over the last two years to address these problems, and this NPR reflects a continued high-level commitment to their implementation.

The Task Force on DoD Nuclear Weapons Management generated a large set of recommendations to the Secretary of Defense and the Military Departments. The Secretary of Defense strongly endorsed the recommendations and took steps in 2008 to ensure their timely implementation. U.S. Strategic Command initiated several efforts to address these findings and to ensure a renewed and sustained dedication, to and focus on, the strategic deterrence mission. The U.S. Navy has been focused on continuous improvement of the nuclear enterprise for more than twenty years; most recently evidenced by the establishment of the Nuclear Weapons Senior Leadership Council and OPNAV Nuclear Weapons Council. The U.S. Air Force roadmap titled "Reinvigorating the Nuclear Enterprise" describes ongoing efforts, including the standing-up of the new Air Force Global Strike Command for nuclear-capable bombers and ICBMs, the consolidation of nuclear sustainment efforts in Air Force Materiel Command and the establishment of the Headquarters, U.S. Air Force Assistant Chief of Staff, Strategic Deterrence and Nuclear Integration (HAF/A10).

Defense Secretary Robert M. Gates tells Airmen at Minot Air Force Base that the Air Force's nuclear mission and maintaining its long tradition of excellence are vital to the security of the United States during a visit Dec. 1, 2008. U.S. Air Force photo by Senior Airman Joe Rivera.

Maintaining leadership focus, expertise, and excellence on nuclear capabilities is a fundamental obligation of the Department of Defense. As the United States reduces the role and numbers of nuclear weapons, sustaining a cadre of talented and expert leaders will become more, not less, important.

LOOKING AHEAD: TOWARD A WORLD WITHOUT NUCLEAR WEAPONS

The U.S. nuclear posture is pivotal to international and national security. While the risk of all-out nuclear war is much diminished relative to the Cold War, nuclear dangers persist and some are increasing. Even as we seek a future world free of nuclear weapons, we are realistic about the world around us, recognizing that this goal will be a long-term effort, not the work of one Administration.

During the Cold War, our nuclear weapons policies and forces were designed to meet two core goals: to deter a massive nuclear or large-scale conventional, biological, or chemical attack by the Soviet Union and its allies; and to reassure our allies and partners that they could count on us to carry out that mission effectively. At the peak of the Cold War, the United States had over 30,000 nuclear weapons, including thousands deployed in overseas locations on short-range delivery systems. The U.S. nuclear weapons production complex constantly developed new types of weapons.

Today, the reassurance mission remains, but the deterrence challenge is fundamentally different. While we must maintain stable deterrence with major nuclear powers, the likelihood of major nuclear war has declined significantly; thus far fewer nuclear weapons are needed to meet our traditional deterrence and reassurance goals. Further, the United States today has the strongest conventional military forces in the world. Our close allies and partners field much of the rest of the world's military power. Moreover, our most pressing security challenge at present is preventing nuclear proliferation and nuclear terrorism, for which a nuclear force of thousands of weapons has little relevance.

As a result of these changes, nuclear weapons play a much more circumscribed role in U.S. national security strategy, a change reflected in the U.S. nuclear posture today. Since the end of the Cold War two decades ago, the United States has cut deployed strategic weapons by approximately 75 percent and has also substantially reduced the overall nuclear stockpile of deployed and non-deployed weapons. As this NPR report makes clear, more can and must be done.

A key focus of the 2010 NPR was therefore to bring our nuclear weapons policies and force posture into better alignment with today's national security priorities. To that end, the NPR decided on a number of steps, many of which have already been initiated or will be pursued in the near term:

- Pursue rigorous measures to reinvigorate the Nuclear Non-Proliferation Treaty (NPT) and the broader non-proliferation regime, and secure vulnerable nuclear materials worldwide against theft or seizure by terrorists;

- Seek ratification and entry into force of the Comprehensive Nuclear Test Ban Treaty and prompt commencement of negotiations on a verifiable Fissile Material Cutoff Treaty;

- Increase efforts to improve nuclear forensics to attribute the source of any covert nuclear attack, so that the United States can hold accountable any state, terrorist group, or other non-state actor that supports or enables terrorist efforts to obtain or use nuclear weapons;

- Adopt a strengthened "negative security assurance" declaring that the United States will not use or threaten to use nuclear weapons against non-nuclear weapon states that are party to the NPT and in compliance with their nuclear non-proliferation obligations;

- Seek ratification and implementation of the New Strategic Arms Reduction Treaty (New START) requiring substantial reductions in deployed U.S. and Russian nuclear forces;

- Structure the reduced U.S. force in a way that promotes stability, including "de-MIRVing" U.S. ICBMs;

- Eliminate the Tomahawk, nuclear-equipped, sea-launched cruise missile (TLAM-N);

- Strengthen regional security architectures and reinforce security commitments to allies and partners by maintaining an effective nuclear umbrella while placing increased reliance on non-nuclear deterrence capabilities (e.g., missile defenses and conventional long-range missiles);

- Work with NATO Allies on a new Strategic Concept that supports Alliance cohesion and sustains effective extended deterrence, while reflecting the role of nuclear weapons in supporting Alliance strategy in the 21st century;

- Pursue high-level dialogues with Russia and China to promote more stable, transparent, and non-threatening strategic relationships between those countries and the United States;

- Continue to posture U.S. forces and enhance command and control arrangements to reduce further the possibility of nuclear weapons launches resulting from accidents, unauthorized actions, or misperceptions and to maximize the time available to the President to consider whether to authorize the use of nuclear weapons;

- Implement well-funded stockpile management and infrastructure investment plans that can sustain a safe, secure, and effective nuclear arsenal at significantly reduced stockpile levels without nuclear testing or the development of new nuclear warheads;

- Complete the Presidentially-directed review of post-New START arms control objectives, to establish goals for future reductions in nuclear weapons, as well as evaluating additional options to increase warning and decision time, and to further reduce the risks of false warning or misjudgments relating to nuclear use; and

- Initiate a comprehensive national research and development program to support continued progress toward a world free of nuclear weapons, including expanded work on verification technologies.

This agenda encompasses a comprehensive set of concrete steps to reduce nuclear dangers to the United States and our allies and partners, to reduce the role and numbers of U.S. nuclear weapons, and at the same time to ensure that nuclear deterrence remains effective for the problems for which it is relevant in today's world.

While the 2010 NPR focused principally on the near term, it also identified a number of longer-term steps to limit nuclear dangers, reduce the role and numbers of U.S. nuclear weapons, and strengthen deterrence of potential adversaries and assurance of U.S. allies and partners. As such, the NPR identified several important objectives toward which the United States should direct future efforts:

- Engage Russia, after ratification and entry into force of New START, in negotiations aimed at achieving substantial further nuclear force reductions and transparency that would cover all nuclear weapons – deployed and non-deployed, strategic and non-strategic;

- Adopt expanded measures to broaden cooperation and transparency, and strengthen strategic stability with Russia and China;

- Continue efforts to strengthen regional security architectures and eliminate chemical and biological weapons, so that over time all states possessing nuclear weapons can be secure in making deterrence of nuclear attack the sole purpose of nuclear weapons;

- Continue to ensure that the United States sustains a safe, secure, and effective nuclear arsenal as long as nuclear weapons exist;

- Following substantial further nuclear force reductions with Russia, engage other states possessing nuclear weapons, over time, in a multilateral effort to limit, reduce, and eventually eliminate all nuclear weapons worldwide;

- Improve nuclear physical infrastructure and human capital to position the United States to safely reduce nuclear weapons, and if international conditions allow, eliminate them altogether. In a world where nuclear weapons had been eliminated but nuclear knowledge remains, having a strong infrastructure and base of human capital would be essential to deterring cheating or breakout, or, if deterrence failed, responding in a timely fashion; and

President Barack Obama and Russian President Dmitry Medvedev sign documents on nuclear arms reduction at the Kremlin in Moscow, Jul. 6, 2009. Official White House photo by Chuck Kennedy.

- Set a course for the verified elimination of all nuclear weapons and minimize risk of cheating and breakout, through increasing transparency and investments in verification technologies focused on nuclear warheads, rather than delivery vehicles.

Toward a World Free of Nuclear Weapons

The long-term goal of U.S. policy is the complete elimination of nuclear weapons. At this point, it is not clear when this goal can be achieved. Pursuing these NPR recommendations will strengthen the security of the United States and its allies and partners and bring us significant steps closer to the President's vision of a world without nuclear weapons.

While security arrangements including NATO will retain a nuclear dimension so long as nuclear threats to the United States and our allies and partners remain, we will continue to seek to reduce the role and numbers of nuclear weapons in the future. In the coming years, as U.S. and allied non-nuclear and counter-WMD capabilities continue to improve and regional security architectures are strengthened, and as we assess progress in restraining other threats, including in particular biological weapons, the United States will consult with allies and partners regarding the conditions under which it would be prudent to shift to a policy under which deterring nuclear attack is the sole purpose of U.S. nuclear weapons.

The conditions that would ultimately permit the United States and others to give up their nuclear weapons without risking greater international instability and insecurity are very demanding. Among those are the resolution of regional disputes that can motivate rival states to acquire and maintain nuclear weapons, success in halting the proliferation of nuclear weapons, much greater transparency into the programs and capabilities of key countries of concern, verification methods and technologies capable of detecting violations of disarmament obligations, and enforcement measures strong and credible enough to deter such violations. Clearly, such conditions do not exist today. But we can – and must – work actively to create those conditions.

The Administration is committed to establishing a sustainable bipartisan consensus on an agenda for American leadership to reduce nuclear risks to ourselves, our allies and partners, and the international community. Together, we can take practical steps immediately and in the near term – starting with those identified in the 2010 NPR – that not only move us toward the ultimate goal of eliminating all nuclear weapons worldwide but can, in their own right, reinvigorate the global nuclear non-proliferation regime, erect higher barriers to the acquisition of nuclear weapons and nuclear materials by terrorist groups, and strengthen U.S. and international security.